THE
CREATIVE LIFE

By Julia Cameron

BOOKS IN THE ARTIST'S WAY SERIES

The Artist's Way
Walking in This World
Finding Water
The Complete Artist's Way
The Artist's Way Workbook
The Artist's Way Every Day

OTHER BOOKS ON CREATIVITY

The Writing Diet
The Right to Write
The Sound of Paper
The Vein of Gold
The Artist's Way Morning Pages Journal
The Artist's Date Book (illustrated by Elizabeth Cameron)
How to Avoid Making Art (or Anything Else You Enjoy)
(illustrated by Elizabeth Cameron)
Supplies: A Troubleshooting Guide for Creative Difficulties
(illustrated by Elizabeth Cameron)
Inspirations: Meditations from The Artist's Way
The Writer's Life: Insights from The Right to Write
The Artist's Way at Work (with Mark Bryan and Catherine Allen)
Money Drunk, Money Sober (with Mark Bryan)

PRAYER BOOKS

Answered Prayers
Heart Steps
Blessings
Transitions
Prayers to the Great Creator

THE
CREATIVE LIFE

True Tales of Inspiration

JULIA CAMERON

JEREMY P. TARCHER/PENGUIN
a member of Penguin Group (USA) Inc.
New York

JEREMY P. TARCHER/PENGUIN
Published by the Penguin Group
Penguin Group (USA) Inc., 375 Hudson Street, New York, New York 10014,
USA • Penguin Group (Canada), 90 Eglinton Avenue East, Suite 700, Toronto,
Ontario M4P 2Y3, Canada (a division of Pearson Penguin Canada Inc.) • Penguin
Books Ltd, 80 Strand, London WC2R 0RL, England • Penguin Ireland, 25 St
Stephen's Green, Dublin 2, Ireland (a division of Penguin Books Ltd) • Penguin
Group (Australia), 707 Collins Street, Melbourne, Victoria 3008, Australia
(a division of Pearson Australia Group Pty Ltd) • Penguin Books India Pvt Ltd, 11
Community Centre, Panchsheel Park, New Delhi–110 017, India • Penguin Group
(NZ), 67 Apollo Drive, Rosedale, Auckland 0632, New Zealand (a division of
Pearson New Zealand Ltd) • Penguin Books, Rosebank Office Park, 181 Jan Smuts
Avenue, Parktown North 2193, South Africa • Penguin China, B7 Jaiming Center,
27 East Third Ring Road North, Chaoyang District, Beijing 100020, China

Penguin Books Ltd, Registered Offices: 80 Strand, London WC2R 0RL, England

First trade paperback edition 2012
Copyright © 2010 by Julia Cameron

Most Tarcher/Penguin books are available at special quantity discounts for bulk
purchase for sales promotions, premiums, fund-raising, and educational needs. Special
books or book excerpts also can be created to fit specific needs. For details, write
Penguin Group (USA) Inc. Special Markets, 375 Hudson Street, New York, NY 10014.

The Library of Congress catalogued the hardcover edition as follows:

Cameron, Julia.
The creative life: true tales of inspiration / Julia Cameron.
p.   cm.
ISBN 978-1-58542-824-3
1. Cameron, Julia.   2. Authors, American—20th century—biography.
3. Creation (Literary, artistic, etc.).   I. Title.
PS3553.A4333A3   2010   2010019956
818'.5409—dc22

ISBN 978-0-399-16052-3 (paperback edition)

Printed in the United States of America
1   3   5   7   9   10   8   6   4   2

BOOK DESIGN BY AMANDA DEWEY

To my colleagues and collaborators, artists all

Acknowledgments

Tyler Beattie

Sophy Burnham

Sara Carder

Sonia Choquette

Steven Fales

Tim Farrington

Joel Fotinos

Chaim Freiberg

Natalie Goldberg

Gerard Hackett

John Herrera

Jack Hofsiss

Linda Kahn

Emma Lively

Susan Raihofer

Domenica Cameron-Scorsese

THE
CREATIVE LIFE

Where to begin? It's a dim, gray day with rain threatening. I sit curled in my big leather writing chair. I am writing longhand, the better to craft an intimate, handmade book. I could go more quickly on a computer, but "quickly" is the villain. For half a year, my life has rushed past, leaving me feeling buffeted. I don't enjoy a speeded-up life. There is no time for savoring people or events. "Aha," says my girlfriend Jennifer Bassey, an actress. "That is the price of success."

I want to throw the brakes on. The price of success strikes me as too high to pay. I want time to walk, not run. I'd go so far as to say I want time to dawdle. Instead of priding myself on the velocity of my life, I want to turn each moment to the light, cradling time like a fine Fabergé egg—or perhaps a crystal casting shards of light on my life. I want to be "in the now," not rushing ahead to a hectic future, not pining for the past, gilded by nostalgia.

On my emotional compass, I want to find myself facing north. For this to happen, I need the input and support of my friends. Left to my own devices, I just spin around. We have the expression "Everything went south." I want to avoid that possibility. And so I seek the companionship of like-minded spirits—people who are both tough-minded and tenderhearted.

Seeking to savor my life, I need to savor first of all my relationships. Friends keep me on track, and yet often I find myself "too busy" to make time for cherishing my friendships. I think of a beloved, but I don't pick up the phone. I don't take pen to page and drop a note. Instead, I hurry forward, and my friendships get cast aside. This carelessness impoverishes my life. I find myself lonely and alone.

Surrounded by people, I too often keep my own

counsel. I do not ask for guidance—I try to muster through myself. My thoughts are often jumbled and hectic. The trail ahead of me seems blocked by conflict.

"Breathe God in and breathe Julia out," advises my friend Jane Cecil, another fine actress, well schooled in living the moment at hand. And so I take a deep breath, trying to fill my lungs with oxygen and my life with gratitude. Gratitude slows down the pace. Gratitude renders the glass half full. If I pause long enough to take a conscious breath, yes, I am grateful. And yet, perched at my window, watching the non-rain, I feel isolated and alone. Yes, everything is fine. It's just hurtling by too fast.

The pell-mell rush of events includes the progress of several musicals representing a decade's worth of work. Last fall, there was a production of one of them, *The Medium at Large*, in Chicago. The production attracted a producer, a director, and an investor. So far so good. In fact, wonderful. Unfortunately, we live in New York, while they all live in Chicago, and so it is to Chicago that my collaborator Emma Lively and I had to go. In Chicago, there were people to see, meetings to be had, places to go, and nowhere near enough sleep. Life was a whirlwind. I couldn't keep up with it.

Putting my pen to the page, I begin to understand my own culpability: I hadn't put first things first. Days passed in which no writing was done. Writing now, I glance out the window at the soft, gray fog, and I begin to find it beautiful. All that is required for this transformation is my focused attention. If I slow down, life is beautiful.

Why not slow down? Half a year has hurtled past me, but I still have half a year left to savor moment by moment. That is what I will do. I will string together the beautiful beads that make up my life. I will slow down and savor my days as they unfurl. I will keep a diary of sorts, with vignettes of my everyday life. Slowing down and paying attention to particular moments, people, and feelings will help me to appreciate them—not to take them for granted. The artist's life can be tumultuous, and yet I chose it—and choose it again on a daily basis. So much of our mythology around creativity portrays the artist as a loner. The truth is far more colorful. Instead of being a solo act, the artist's life involves many. It could be said that "it takes a village." Meeting my "village" will help the reader to identify his own.

Today is a limbo day. Manhattan is wreathed in fog, and drops of moisture accumulate on my fire escape. It is not raining, but it's certainly not dry. It is a bad hair day. Pedestrians walk hunched forward, umbrellas at the ready. Everyone is under the weather. I tell myself I am too crabby to write, but I know that writing will relieve my crabbiness. I can write myself into a sunny mood. At the very least, I can try.

The early night sky is cobalt blue. The lights of Manhattan gleam silver and gold. The fog has cleared, and tomorrow promises sunshine and warmth. My day tomorrow looms empty of commitments. It's a day to write. But tonight, too, is a time to write. It feels good to debrief in writing. So what is there to report? I am tucked into my bedroom in a large, sunny apartment containing three separate wings: one for me; one for my roommate, colleague, and collaborator, Emma Lively; and one for guests. The apartment is big— the guest wing doubles as an office and library—but I find myself working best from the cozy corner of my bedroom. There I have my writing chair and a small Oriental desk.

For ten days now we've had a houseguest—Tyler Beattie, a young and brilliant director. Tyler came to town to help Emma stage a reading of her musical *Bunny's Bakery*. Working at warp speed, they flew through several drafts. Then Tyler assembled a gifted cast from among his friends, Northwestern alumni. With only two days to learn the music, they came through with flying colors. The reading was a tremendous success, garnering a standing ovation from the assembled crowd. Emma and Tyler took their bows with glee and relief written across their faces.

"They really liked it!" Emma repeated to me with wonder.

"They really liked it," I assured her back.

From the reading, Emma and Tyler went straight to recording a demo. They wanted to catch lightning in a bottle. The recording was expensive but well worth it. It would be the calling card for Emma and Tyler's songwriting talents. I told Emma it was as though she had hoisted a flag that was lettered "I'm brilliant."

"You think so?" she asked, although a part of her knew that it was true.

"Yes," I told her. "The show is fine. Don't go fixing it. There's nothing much to fix."

The cobalt sky has darkened to inky black. Tyler takes to the piano, rippling the keys with a song from *Avalon*, the musical we are set to work on next. *Avalon* was my very first musical, which has rested dormant for nearly ten years. It is the first show Emma wrote on, and it sounds both naïve and fresh. We are much more skilled now than we were a decade ago. It's time to build on what's good and discard the rest. Tyler's fresh eyes are a godsend.

"What if I try this to make it less Gilbert and Sullivan?" Tyler asks. He deftly alters the music as written to something more modern. I feel a wave of excitement. *Avalon* may have a life after all.

In talking to Sharee Pemberton, our producer, I once received the compliment, "You and Emma are so prolific." I think to myself that the secret lies in never throwing anything away. What we can't master today, we might well master tomorrow. Our skills may catch up to our vision after all. At the moment, we have tabled our show *Magellan*. When we return to it, we will know more. Working with Tyler is good for us. He has great detachment. Having him help us with *Avalon* is like assisting a skilled surgeon during a tricky operation. How to keep *Avalon* fresh but not naïve is the question. It is too repetitious, and Tyler wants to fold multiple songs together.

It's nearly midnight. Tyler still has plenty of energy—he's twenty-three. Emma, too, can muster more wind. I am the one who is too tired to think well, and so I fold my hand.

"More tomorrow," I promise Tyler, who reluctantly abandons the keys.

"More tomorrow," I promise Emma.

The day is clear, bright, and sunny. Our apartment is flooded with light and music. Tyler is at the keys working his way through *Avalon*.

"What about this?" he asks as he plays.

"I think it needs to be lighter, with more of a pop feel," Emma ventures. She holds a master's degree in viola performance but feels her true voice lies in writing for Broadway.

"Maybe like this?" Tyler shifts gears.

"That's it exactly," I pipe up with excitement.

"It's a little 'Disney princess,'" notes Tyler.

"Yes, I guess it is," I say. "That's not a bad thing, is it?"

"The show, as it's written now, is very classical," Tyler answers. "The direction you want to go in is more pop."

"I think the little priestess's songs should still have a magical feel," I say.

"You mean like this?" Tyler asks, shifting gears again.

"Yes, that's it!"

Working with Tyler makes me dizzy. He has more gears than a racing bike. Moving song to song and gear to gear, he brings *Avalon* to fresh life. Emma and I have high hopes for the show. It is so full of promise. As it stands, it's halfway terrific and halfway flawed.

Tyler sees the job as one of paring down the number of melodies, holding on to the best of them and letting go of the rest. We have enough music for three shows, he says. I see this now and laugh. Writing *Avalon*, I put in every-thing but the kitchen sink. I was so excited to be writing music that I didn't know when to stop. I was living in Lon-don, and songs seemed to hang in the air. In a two-month period, I wrote sixty pieces of music.

Our job now is to pick the best. Surprisingly, Emma, Tyler, and I seem to concur on just which songs to choose. We make an outline of the show, noting which songs go where. The good of the old show survives, but the outline points to new directions. Emma and I have our work cut out for us. Tyler will head to Connecticut to direct a show there. In two weeks, he'll return to check on our progress.

When I first wrote *Avalon*, I wanted the show to be mine, all mine. When Emma joined forces, it became clear she deserved credit. Now with Tyler aboard, it is time to share credit again. It is more important that the show have a life than it is to have solo credit. In the ten years since the show was conceived, I have become more realistic and more generous. When we tell Tyler he will be getting credit, he is both thrilled and surprised.

"Now I'll really dive into the work," he says. It feels good to have his fresh energy. It feels good to have *Avalon* getting onto its feet after a decade on the shelf.

"I love this show," I tell Emma and Tyler. "It may be a mess right now, but it's a great mess."

Resuscitating *Avalon* brings home to me the value of collaborating. Left to my own devices, the show would remain flawed and on the shelf. With the help of Emma and Tyler, the show goes forward. They see what I don't. The show lurches to its feet, and we begin cutting and pasting. Three villains are pared down to two. The secondary characters' love duet is moved from Act One to deep in Act

Two. The heroine steps forward with an "I want" song. In the eleven-o'clock song, she gets her wish. The finale tags all bases and closes the show with a bang.

I am learning again the lesson of work and rework. My novel *Mozart's Ghost* underwent nine drafts and forty-three submissions. Working on its sequel, I was prepared to write and rewrite. As the drafts mounted, I could see and feel improvement. Why should it be different with a musical? The key to success obviously lies with open-mindedness. It's better by far to be willing to change and improve a piece of work than to stubbornly insist on its genius. The longer I write, the more open I am to other people's ideas. I have a trusted cache of friends who read my early drafts and make suggestions. I have a smart and driven literary agent who also weighs in. I work with an editor who comments tersely on my already rewritten drafts. Taken as a group, my friends and colleagues have a certain tough-minded optimism. They believe in my work and believe, also, that it can be made better. All it takes is the humility to try again. And so, listening to Tyler's notes as well as Emma's, I send *Avalon* through the rewrite cycle one more time.

"So you will rework the book and then we'll rendez-vous in ten days to work on the music," Tyler proposes.

"That sounds good," Emma answers.

The bright sun passes behind a cloud. The temporary darkness matches my mood—I am willing to work again, but I wish I didn't have to. Ah, but I do. *Avalon*'s theme song states, "Just close your eyes and you'll see it. Just cross the bridge and it's there." Obedient, I go to work. "Open your heart, that's the place you must start . . ." I strive for an open heart.

New York taxicabs now feature something called "Taxi TV." There is a screen that features *Eyewitness News*, and that news includes a "meteorologist's report" on the weather. The report spotlights five days' weather at a crack. We're due for five days' rain, according to the projection. Somehow knowing what's to come only makes it feel worse. Rain? Yes, it is raining.

Tyler has gone to Connecticut, leaving Emma in tears at his departure. "He'll be back soon," I assure her, but she is inconsolable. She loves collaborating with him and feels that she has done some of her best work in tandem with Tyler.

"Don't worry. He'll be back soon," I tell her. "You're Muses for each other."

"I need a day to metabolize things," Emma declares. Of course she does. She went from working on *Bunny's Bakery* with all the tumult of success and congratulations to working on *Avalon* with all of its marred brilliance. Like me, Emma stands ready to work but exhausted. A day of rest is clearly called for. A rainy day of rest is at hand.

Emma and I have been working together for more than eleven years. She came to work for me as a literary assistant, but within six months she was hard at work on the musicals. According to Emma, I dangled the musicals as a carrot when I hired her. I don't remember doing that, but perhaps I did.

To hear Emma tell it, her going to work on the musicals was like something out of a fairy tale. "I can play music, but I don't know how to arrange it," she remembers lamenting.

"I have no sympathy for you," I replied, locking her in a room with a piano. The moment the door latched, she began hearing music, and she has continued hearing music ever since. At first, she was content to harmonize my melodies. Now she hears melodies of her own.

"I always wanted to be a composer," she says, recalling a childhood dream. "I just never thought it was possible."

But it was—and is—possible. Emma's gift for melody fills the house with music. She wakes up eager to get to the keys, and she often works a long day that doesn't end until nightfall. For my part, I go to the keys and chase down melodies that I am hearing. "Emma," I sometimes call, "listen to this!" Emma jots down the melody that she will flesh out later. So far, she has not tired of my melodies, nor I of hers.

"More tomorrow," Emma calls out. A sudden boom of thunder sets Charlotte, her little West Highland terrier, to shaking. Emma scoops her in her arms. "It's OK, Charlotte," she tells her as a bolt of lightning illuminates the skyline. "It's OK, it's OK," she repeats. Charlotte will not stop shaking until the storm has passed.

The relentless rain has broken. The sky is still gray and walkers carry their umbrellas at the ready. It has rained seventeen out of the last twenty-one days, a record amount of rainfall. Central Park is lush and green. A stiff breeze makes the trees sway like underwater plants.

Working as a trio, Emma, Tyler, and I have pulled *Avalon* apart and then put the show back together again. We've eliminated musical repetition and punched up the lyrics. Today, Saturday, Emma is typing up a draft of the show to have it ready for a reading Monday night. Faced with the reading, I am nervous. Will the show hold up? I hope so.

For Monday night's reading, we will have a small crowd of musical theater professionals. Ours will not be the roughest script they've heard, nor will it be the most polished. It is very much a work in progress. Honing it is a process. Readings will demand further readings. Book, lyrics, and music all will come under scrutiny. Musicals are perhaps the most demanding art form that I practice. And "practice" is precisely the right word.

I have been writing full-time for forty-three years, ever since I was eighteen. At the beginning of my writing, I tried to write final drafts. I didn't understand the value of rough drafts. Everything I wrote had to be polished, perfect. I slaved over each paragraph. At age twenty-nine, I got sober. I began to practice "one day at a time" and "easy does it." With sobriety came a new way of writing. I wrote daily, and I wrote sensible amounts. Rough drafts became part of my writing practice. I learned to lighten up and allow myself the freedom to make errors. To my surprise,

I found I didn't make too many errors. Rough drafts and final drafts were closer together than I thought. Sometimes my rough drafts actually served as my final drafts. Once I relaxed, my writing became clearer and easier. No longer striving to be brilliant and clever, I began to write more about communication. As I practiced more humility, my work became far more accessible. People liked it better, and I liked it better myself. My ego became less invested in "my" work. As a result, I found myself able to collaborate. I discovered that others had ideas that could strengthen my own. This was a far cry from me as a young writer, who couldn't bear to have a comma changed.

Monday night: the living room is crowded. I perch in a side chair, eager to hear what we have wrought. Emma reads the opening stage directions. The actors launch into their parts. Gone are the repetitions. The script is lean— too lean, I start to think. We have overcut the show. It reads more like a sketch. The running time is sixty-four minutes. Too short. Too fast.

After the read-through we have a question-and-answer session. To my relief, the comments are largely positive, but as I suspected, the viewers want "more." It is a process, I remind myself. Tyler and Emma are well satisfied. The show they began with was long and murky, running close to three hours. Better to need to add than to subtract. After an hour's talk, our guests make their way home.

"Well, we've made some giant strides in the right direction," ventures Tyler.

"The story is clear now," chimes in Emma.

"We've cut some sequences that can go back in now," I say. I don't want to discourage Tyler and Emma, but I feel the lean show lacks heart. I say as much. To my relief, both Emma and Tyler are open to my thoughts. They are good collaborators, far better than I was at their ages. We agree to give the show a few days' rest until we start again.

"It's a process," Emma reminds us all. The phrase is becoming a mantra.

It is a Wednesday and the day is bright and clear with a fresh breeze. The temperature is in the mid-seventies, an idyllic temperature for a summer's day. Tonight I will teach down in SoHo at the Open Center. I've been teaching for a month, enduring summer rainstorms every Wednesday night.

I am teaching a short, intense course on writing. It is named "The Right to Write," after the book it is based on. Students undergo a deep immersion in the tools of a writing life. They write Morning Pages every morning, and by night they work on a narrative timeline: an autobiographical telling of their life. Additionally, they read *The Right to Write* and execute the many tasks the book offers. When we rendezvous for class, they break into clusters of three, checking in on the week's work, then doing some playful writing exercises. They check in with me on Morning Pages, Artist Dates, walks, synchronicity, the narrative timeline, and the tasks of the week. Every group I teach has an individual persona. This crew is particularly intense, plagued by the issue of perfectionism. We work weekly at the dismantling of perfectionism and the development of spontaneity.

Ordinarily, Wednesday is not a writing day for me. My day's Morning Pages usually urge me to focus on my teaching, not my writing. This Wednesday, today, I will be teaching about mood, about the fact that you don't need to be "in the mood" in order to write. A writer's relationship to writing resembles a marriage. Just as a long-term couple may not feel like making love until the first caress leads to the next, for a writer the first sentence on a page often leads to other sentences. Some of the finest writing gets done when we're "not in the mood."

Wednesday night: this class is volatile. I feel the tension in the room, and so I ask, "How many people are grumpy tonight?" The hands shoot up; fully two-thirds of the class call themselves grumpy. I break them into clusters to let them vent. Fifteen minutes pass and the tone of the room shifts decisively. There are staccato bursts of laughter. "Grumpy" begins to evaporate. I suspect that perfectionism was once again to blame. Individually, they tend to set the bar too high, putting undue pressure on themselves. Working in clusters, hearing the experience of others, the class begins to relax. They see that while they may not have worked perfectly, they have indeed made strides.

We play a game called "popcorn," in which the members of the class give one another positive feedback. Deceptively simple, the game is revolutionary. Before this class, the group was accustomed to receiving only negative feedback to "fix" their writing. Now they are asked to focus on the positive, telling one another the good that they heard. They feed one another such comments as "You're very funny" or "You're really adventurous." Listening more closely, they may weigh in with "You've got a great ear for dialogue" or "You've got a powerful sense of place." As they seek to build on these positives, each student's writing grows stronger. Feeling their writing connect with readers, students gain encouragement. Laughter increases, rippling through the room. "How many people are still grumpy?" I ask. This time, the question is greeted by laughter. No hands shoot into the air. I have explained to my students the value of Believing Mirrors—people who see our power and potential and reflect it back to us—but now they are experiencing their value firsthand.

In 12-step jargon we are told, "You're only as sick as your secrets." Many of us harbor secrets around our creativity. Harsh criticism moved one young writer I know to contemplate suicide. "The window started calling to me," she said, relating her dark hour. "What if I never make it?" she asked. Listening to her, I was glad she had chosen me to share her secret with. Just talking it out made it far less likely that she would act on her impulse to self-destruct.

"I'm so ashamed of myself," the young writer told me. "I was embarrassed to tell anyone, even you, how I was feeling."

"It's good you told me. It siphons some of the poison out," I told her. "From my perspective, you've got a good career, and if you keep at it, it will be a long and fruitful one to boot."

The young writer listened to me with skepticism. The damning criticism had shaken her confidence. Not only did the critic reject her work, he had added that everyone else would probably reject her work, too. I tried to point out that this was sheer nonsense—one person's opinion. The very next day, the young writer got a glowing report from a veteran director who pronounced her work "delight-ful," adding that she was "clearly a talent to be watched." I watched the young writer try to take in the positive. On any reasonable scale, the veteran director's comments should have weighed heavily, but for the young writer, the critic's negatives still held sway.

"Talk it out," I urged. "Don't bottle it up. Don't make the rejection your secret." Reluctantly, the young writer placed phone calls to two Believing Mirrors.

"It's just one person being negative," her first friend reassured her. "Everyone else has been positive."

"You're projecting," she was told by her second friend. "And what you are projecting is disaster. Stay in the now. The now is all we've got."

"I had a moment of clarity then," the young writer told me. "I realized that I was probably in the best position of my life. I may not yet have all that I want, but I have far more than I've ever had previously."

The young writer's shift of perspective came about from sharing the devastation that harsh criticism had caused her. Using her Believing Mirrors, she was restored to sanity.

I live on the Upper West Side of Manhattan, which is a relaxed and casual place. When I venture to the Upper East Side, I always feel underdressed. So tonight I dress with special care. I am headed to an East Side restaurant, meeting my friend Peter Lewis. He is not a vegetarian, but he loves vegetarian food, so that is the fare for the evening. I will order something named "the Zen platter," featuring tofu, seitan, and collard greens. The meal is tasty, but the real point of the evening is Peter's new adventure. He has enrolled in a beginning acting class and has received his first scene to prepare, a five-page excerpt from Arthur Miller's *All My Sons*.

"It's a great scene," Peter says enthusiastically. "I play the father. He's a man with a terrible secret."

We place our orders and then settle in to read the scene. I play Peter's son. The son wants the father to acknowledge that his brother had been killed in an airplane crash three years earlier. Little does he realize that the father's factory manufactured the defective parts that may have caused the crash. The boy's mother, Peter's wife, still holds out hope that the son has survived the plane crash somehow and will appear at any moment. This is a delusional fantasy, the son feels. Further, he wants to marry the girl once spoken for by the missing brother. The father protests that such a marriage would shatter the mother's heart.

Peter starts the scene from memory, and I chime in, reading the part of his son. Peter plays the scene with a tough edge. His secret guilt causes him to be gruff. We play the scene once through and pause to eat our salads. Before our entrées come, we have time to run the scene again.

Peter is settling into his part. His hidden pain comes out as a rasp in his voice. Not only is his son dead: he may have killed him. Now he stands to lose the surviving son unless he agrees to confront his wife with her delusion. At the very thought of such a confrontation, the father chokes up. Playing him, Peter gets a catch in his throat. The idea of disabusing his wife of her fantasy is too much for him. Father and son reach a standoff. The scene ends.

"From what I gather," says Peter, "you have to know your lines absolutely cold. That frees you up to listen and react to your partner." Peter knows his lines close to cold. He enjoys running the scene with me, but he is frustrated that his scene partner refuses to get together to work on the scene. "So he expects we'll just show up and do it." Peter snaps. "Just like that."

Our entrées arrive, and Peter picks at his food. The scene lies on the table between us. We run it two more times in place of dessert. Secure in his lines, Peter kicks into character and stays there. I have the disquieting experience of losing my friend's company and meeting a stranger.

"Peter, I think you're going to be good," I finally interject.

"You think so? Yeah, maybe," answers Peter, coming back to Peter. He stuffs the pages of the scene into his briefcase.

Saturday night: I am set to rendezvous with Peter and learn how his scene went. We meet at the vegetarian restaurant where the waiter greets us as the regulars we are becoming.

"You first," Peter urges. "Tell me about *Avalon*."

I tell him what I think: that *Avalon* had gotten overcut and that we needed to restore some sequences.

"Well, it's a process," Peter says, echoing Emma.

"Yes, I know that," I answer, somewhat defensively. "And your scene?" I ask.

"I didn't drop any lines. I didn't grind the scene to a halt. They said that I was too up in my head, not enough in the moment," Peter dolefully reports.

"Ah, well, it's a process," I tell him. That phrase again!

"It's a process," he echoes.

I think how good we are at diagnosing each other's creative difficulties. We urge gentleness on each other: advice it's easy to give and hard to follow. If only I could accept that reworking *Avalon* is a process, I might share Emma and Tyler's optimism over strides made in the right direction. If only Peter could accept acting as an avenue for gentle learning, he might be encouraged, too. Instead, each of us has his foot to the accelerator. Yes, we want to be good, but we want to be good *now*. We have our eyes on the product and not the process. We know better, but we ignore our knowledge. Like it or not, the next step for both of us is small, not large. Peter needs a scene study class, and I need to work with Emma and Tyler to flesh out the missing sequences.

"Dessert?" the waiter asks us.

"No, thanks, not this time," we both demur. The sweetness we are after is spiritual, not physical. No dollop of sugar will take the place of a job well done. We both need to slow down. And so we do.

"I should find a scene study class," Peter volunteers as we pay the check.

"I should reread the original *Avalon* and work with Emma and Tyler to restore the show's heart."

"So we know what we need to do," Peter concludes, stepping to the curb to hail a cab.

"We do," I say. A taxi swerves across two lanes of traffic. Peter opens the door.

"I'll see you in a week," I say. "Good luck."

"Remember, it's a process," says Peter. He shuts the cab door.

"Where to, lady?" asks the driver. I give him my address.

The day is chill, more like April than July. Puddles stand ankle-deep at the curb. According to the weatherman, it will rain again before it clears. I shove an umbrella into my purse. I have a dinner date, as I do every Tuesday with my longtime friend Tracy Jamar.

I met Tracy thirty years ago when I spotted her riding Western-style in Central Park. Flagging her down, I asked what stable she came from, and that question opened a dialogue that has gone on for three decades. With Tracy's help, I rented and later bought a spirited Appaloosa from Claremont Stables, where Tracy kept her horse, Arrow.

Both of us using Western tack, we rode our horses together around the reservoir in Central Park. Frequently, I brought my daughter, Domenica, up double. She was a mere toddler, and her legs stuck out akimbo. Tracy, by contrast, was the epitome of grace. As we looped the cinder path circling the reservoir, joggers waved us hello, their salutes welcoming us on our rounds. Less welcoming was a flasher who lurked at the northernmost bend. Even from horseback, his was a threatening figure. We cantered past him, knowing that the change in gait would distract Domenica. "Hold on tight, sweetie," I would tell her.

Safely back at the stable, Tracy and I would trade our riding boots for roller skates. This was before Rollerblades came into vogue. Tracy and I were virtually the only skat-ers on the Upper West Side. We'd head off for home; she to the north, me to the south. Both of us enjoyed the sense of danger and adventure the skates afforded us as we dodged through traffic.

But that was thirty years ago.

Now when we meet, we come on foot. She from the north still, loping with long strides the twenty-five blocks to the restaurant. I live a scant block away. We rendez-vous at Jackson Hole, a faux-Western restaurant, featuring Whopper-sized burgers and shakes.

"You look wonderful," I greet Tracy—and she does. Still a leggy beauty now in her mid-fifties, Tracy was the prototype for the man-eating character named "Stacy" in my novel *Mozart's Ghost*. Tracy herself is now happily married to her lover of fifteen years' standing. She wears a large and glorious diamond ring, held in place by a wedding band of diamonds. She has a habit of toying with her rings.

"I've taken some restoration jobs," Tracy announces. She is a museum-caliber expert at needlework, restoring quilts, hooked rugs, and embroidered or needlepointed furniture. Additionally, she hooks contemporary rugs. To hear her tell it, her apartment is overflowing with needle-craft projects and the raw materials for future projects: a cornucopia of creativity.

"I really need to throw some things out," she laments. "My place is really crammed to overflowing."

I know from past experience that Tracy's lament is a prelude to action. It's a sort of creative cha-cha. First complain—one, two—then act on the gripes—cha, cha, cha. For the past three years, I have listened to her grumble about the stress of her degree program at Goddard. She is doing an individualized bachelor of arts program known as the IBA. The grumbling always precedes her gathering her-self together and delivering the paper or project that looms as impossible. "What do they expect?" Tracy's modus operandi might be dubbed "ventilate, then activate." From her example, I have learned the value of articulating creative challenges. Nothing is too petty to bear mention. And the simple act of venting—with humor, if possible—makes me the author of my life.

Making a piece of art requires myriad tiny steps. Grumbling about each of them may well free up the energy to act. One thing it surely does is dismantle the mythology that tells us art is made by loners and made with heroic ease. Based on that false standard, we will always come up short. How much better and how much healthier to admit a need for help and support. How much nicer to rally our resources with our friends' encouragement still ringing in our ears.

I tell Tracy, "My writing feels uphill."

"That's what you usually say," she responds.

This comment comes as a surprise to me. Are all my books difficult? Is writing a book like birthing a baby? You forget the pain and suffering after the fact? Perhaps it's true. Hoping to recapture my writing voice, I have been rereading *The Sound of Paper*. It is a book that seems born of ease, yet there it is in black and white, "It isn't easy, at first, getting our perceptions onto the page. . . . It takes an effort to be clear about things. . . ."

"Just keep writing. It will come easier," Tracy tells me. She sounds certain.

"You mean it's always like this?" I ask her. I can hear my self-pity revving up.

"Well, it's been like this for at least thirty years," she says. "That's long enough that it might seem like a trend."

"So I just need to resign myself?"

"Yes. It's always hard and then it always gets easier." Tracy sounds matter-of-fact.

"I can live with that," I tell her. It occurs to me that writing is like horseback riding. When you start up you are stiff and sore. After a few rides, you are more limber. A few rides after that and it's easy. I tell Tracy my analogy, and she laughs.

"Just don't let the difficulty throw you," she advises. "Stay on the horse."

Yet another gray day. It's not raining, but the weatherman promises we will have showers. Sensing a storm, the little dogs are loath to go out. For them, it's a day for sleeping curled up at the foot of my bed. I myself woke up late, my animal self sleeping in. Last night, I taught the final class of "The Right to Write." Midway through teaching, I received a note passed to the front. "Could we hear more from you?" the note read. "Enough of this business of learning from each other."

The note takes me aback. As a deliberate teaching strategy, I focus the group on itself, not on me. I don't want people fixated on "the magic teacher." I want them to realize their answers lie within them and their peers. Usually, after some initial resistance, a class comes to appreciate the depth of its own resources. So excited are they by the process of clustering in small groups that I can barely get a word in edgewise. They fall in love with themselves as a class. I become almost extraneous.

"What do you want to know?" I ask the class, expect-ing the questions to be deep water. Instead the question comes: "What is your favorite fast-writing pen?"

"Uni-Ball Vision Elite," I answer. "They're made in Japan but are easy to find here."

"How do you move from a first draft to a more pol-ished draft?" comes the next query.

"I submit my rough draft to a set of Believing Mir-rors, people whose feedback I trust. I let them tell me what parts are strongest," I answer.

"What is a recent Artist Date?" a woman in the back row asks me.

"The frog exhibit at the American Museum of Natu-ral History. The prettiest little frogs are deadly poison," I tell her.

"What's a recent synchronicity?" she asks.

"The show *Camelot* being produced just as we needed to rework *Avalon*. Lots of good Merlin lore," I answer.

The questions continue, and I answer them one by one. On the classroom clock, the minute hand inches toward the six, signaling class is at a close. We end with a round of applause: me to them, them to me. "Job well done" is the mutual compliment. It gives me great satisfaction to have given the keys to the kingdom to them.

One of my students is a veteran Broadway actor whom I've known for several years. Writing his narrative timeline, he scooped up a cup of memories about his childhood in Cuba. His writing is vivid and colorful, chock-full of sights and sounds. He tells the story of one Christmas when Santa Claus blundered, giving him a doll and his cousin a fire truck. No, he would not trade presents! No, he would not admit Santa had made a mistake! The doll spoke to his deepest yearnings. Until that moment, he had felt lonely and misunderstood. His story was vibrant and vital—good material for a one-man show.

"I loved it," I told him. I felt a little smug. I had guessed that he would be a strong writer, and I had urged him to take the class. Now my hunch had paid off.

"*Muchas gracias*," my friend answered, his face lit by self-esteem.

"*De nada*," I responded, thinking that the gift of hav-ing unblocked him was the kind of present my Santa Claus might bring.

This afternoon, rain notwithstanding, I will pay a hospital visit to a friend who is in dire straits. A bad cold turned out to be pneumonia. A lung collapsed. He is on oxygen and has undergone a tracheotomy. He endures sleep apnea. For seven weeks, he has been hospitalized. Newly moved out of the ICU, he will receive us as his first visitors. He cannot talk. We will strive to read his lips.

I am afraid, irrationally afraid, of going to the hospital. Like little dog Charlotte, I shake at the prospect. "Give me strength," I pray. "Give me calm." When I wake up, I find I have the serenity of Tiger Lily, my cocker spaniel. I dress serenely in basic black with a single golden brooch.

It is a short cab ride over to the hospital. Once there, it's a maze of hallways, elevators, and more hallways to reach my friend's room. As we approach the room, a nurse stops us and asks that we wear smocks and wash our hands, and that we not touch our ailing friend.

"Is that so we don't give him any more germs?" Emma asks.

"He has an infection," the nurse answers. "The germs go both ways."

We enter the room, warned off hugs and kisses, urged to keep our distance. The warning seems unnecessary faced with our friend prone on his back with tubes sprouting everywhere. We blow him our kisses and he mouths, "I can't talk."

Emma repeats, "You can't talk."

He nods yes. "I didn't sleep last night," he mouths next. "I have sleep apnea."

Once more Emma parrots exactly what he says, then she holds out her iPhone with a picture of Charlotte. Our friend smiles. He loves dogs.

"She misses you," Emma says. Our friend nods, then stifles a groan.

"You need to sleep, don't you?" Emma asks.

"Last night was hard," our friend concurs. "I'm tired."

"Well, we're very glad to have seen you," I interject. "It's been hell missing you."

"Yes. Hell," our friend agrees.

"We'll let you sleep now," says Emma, drawing our brief visit to a close.

"Lots of love," I say.

"Yes." Our friend nods. "Lots of love."

In the taxi riding back home, Emma and I debrief. We are both relieved. Our friend is back from death's door.

"He looked much better than I thought he would," says Emma.

"Yes, he did," I echo. "Of course, it's hard to know how much of his demeanor was 'act as if.' He has a very, very strong will."

We ride the rest of the way home in silence. We will go back again soon.

Tonight the night sky is lit by heat lightning. Distant thunder rumbles. Although it is not yet raining, rain is predicted, and Charlotte, our resident weatherman, confirms the prediction. She is curled at the foot of my bed, shaking in anticipation. No amount of tender words can soothe her. She is convinced the end is nigh. Meanwhile, Tiger Lily is sprawled in the hallway in splendid indifference. Let the storm strike. She is snug and secure. Donning rain gear and grabbing an umbrella, I hurry out.

Tonight, I have dinner with a young film director. First we see *Harry Potter and the Half-Blood Prince*, then we walk north from Columbus Circle to The City Grill, once a favored rendezvous. It is eleven p.m., late enough that the restaurant is half empty. We are shown to a booth and left to peruse our menus. It will be salads, we decide. Salads and lemonade. The waiter takes our orders and retreats toward the kitchen. I notice a blowsy blonde drinking at the bar.

"There but for the grace of God," I exclaim, grateful in my sobriety. That opens the floodgates.

"I had a bumpy week," the young director begins.

"How so?" I ask. Our lemonades arrive.

"I learned that someone was spreading rumors about me."

"Rumors? What sort of rumors?" I know the young director as someone of impeccable character, graceful and self-contained.

"It would seem I am an ex-alcoholic." As he sips at lemonade, the director's eyes fills with tears. "I've decided not to confront the rumormonger. I just won't work with her, and she won't know why."

"What did you say to the person who told you?" I ask.

"I said I wasn't an alcoholic, and I said I went to therapy to learn healthier behaviors."

"It's a shame to have a beautiful part of your life held against you," I say.

"It's no different than being taunted in grammar

school," says the young director. "Fortunately, the people she gossiped to chose not to believe her rumors. They trusted their own impression of me."

"Still, it must have felt horrible."

"It did. I told my friends about it, and one of them bought me a bouquet of flowers."

"That's lovely." Our salads arrive.

"Yes, it felt good."

"It's nice that someone understood how much you were hurt."

"Yes."

Our salads are not very tasty, although possibly our appetites are thrown off by the conversation.

"It's a funny thing. I'm so used to being a sober alcoholic that I am not used to having 'alcoholic' be a bad thing anymore. Most of my friends are sober alcoholics."

"I know." The young director focuses on my feelings. After all, I am the alcoholic at the table.

"I've been around long enough to believe what goes around comes around."

"I'm just glad this happened now, and not on my first day of shooting," says the young director, digging into the Hawaiian salad with grim determination. I admire the decision to do nothing in self-defense. It strikes me as being mature far beyond the director's years. I say as much.

"Thank you. I always wondered how I would handle rumors in my work. Now it's happened and I know."

"You're handling it beautifully," I say, summing up the case. I pick at my salad, then signal for the check. We each lay down a twenty. I feel proud the director has confided in me.

"It feels good to talk it out with a neutral party."

"You're wise not to get into it," I say. "If you take it on, it's just more drama."

"Yes. I try to keep my drama on the screen."

We leave the restaurant, passing the blonde at the bar, who is now visibly drunker. She has attracted the attention of a male drinker. It is easy to predict how the evening will end up.

"But for the grace of God," I say aloud to the young director. We step past.

Great bolts of lightning course across the sky. Deep bellows of thunder shake the air. It's late at night and the storm that was promised is finally striking. As usual, Tiger Lily grows very calm while Charlotte begins shaking. I am beginning to recognize that Tiger Lily's calm is actually an avoidance strategy. If she is just quiet enough maybe the storm will not notice her. She is playing possum.

The storm outside my writing-room window is as bold and vivid as the storms where I used to live out in New Mexico. Here, the mountain peaks are the twin towers of the El Dorado, an apartment building that dominates the Central Park West skyline. Jagged bolts of lightning throw the towers into relief. A high wind sends sheets of rain shearing sideways. Charlotte tucks herself along the flank of my writing chair. She is shaking violently, and will continue to shake until the storm has passed. It's in no hurry to do so.

I am writing under a deadline, and tonight I am thinking that the seasons of creativity pass very much like the passing storm. There are times that are simply difficult, and those times will pass—eventually. My writing will get easier. Just not tonight.

I remind myself of what I know: the trick to surviving difficult times is to admit they are truly difficult. Yet these difficult times will pass. There is no point in fighting the storm or willing it to pass sooner. The storm takes the time it takes. There is no point in pressuring myself. Better to gently encourage my psyche, practicing delight in what I find. The storm is a tutor to me. Its turbulence teaches that I am resilient enough to survive the tumult.

Much of our mythology about creativity centers on drama. Creativity is spoken of in violent terms. We experience a "flash of inspiration," "a sudden breakthrough," "a startling insight." Sometimes creativity is dramatic. More often and more happily, it comes to us with quiet urgency. Our days are calm and our creativity bubbles along like a gentle stream, delightful but not dramatic. The key to being prolific is steady production. It works well to set a modest daily quotient, one that can be met without too much strain. For me, the daily quotient is three pages.

A jagged bolt of lightning flashes horizontally across the sky. The Hudson River glitters in its light. The storm seems centered directly west of Manhattan. Then the storm stalks closer on lightning lags. A bolt at a time, it walks across the river until it is directly overhead near Central Park. Now bolts of light illuminate the reservoir. Its surface shines like shook foil. Charlotte quivers as if each bolt is an arrow aimed directly at her. Tiger Lily lies very, very still. Pen in hand, I set words to the page. I strive to be steady and productive despite the drama of the storm.

"Charlotte, it's really all right," I address the shaking little dog. Her trembling continues unabated.

"I'm going to go to bed now, Charlotte," I tell her. I make a place for her at the foot of my bed. She slinks past it to a pile of pillows. Perched at the top of the pile, she stares out the window, keeping sentinel on the storm.

I feel like writing, but I am afraid I have lost my voice. Sentences swim to me, only to be shot down by my Inner Censor. This is a creature who is never happy, never satis-fied with my work. I call him Nigel, and I visualize him as a gay British designer. Nothing I ever do will quite match Nigel's standards. He is the one who is hissing in my ear that my writing voice is lost—not that he thought much of my voice to begin with.

We're having another downpour, but Nigel doesn't think much of my ability to describe it. Thunder rumbles like a troupe of Harley-Davidsons. Lightning flashes like a strobe. One more time the dogs are at their antics. Tiger Lily dead calm, Charlotte shaking. I have just read an issue of W from cover to cover. One of the articles I read was about Christopher Buckley, who has just penned a memoir about his famous deceased parents, Pat and William F. Buckley.

In the article I learned that Pat Buckley was an inveterate tippler, while William F. was prone to popping pills. Pat was fond of wine—too fond, the article hinted—although it stopped short of calling her an alcoholic. The portrait of the celebrated couple had them barely speaking to each other much of the time. Their son, Christopher, seems almost an afterthought, a fact he grappled with by writing the memoir. Celebrated though his parents were in life, in death he had the last word.

For me, finding out that William F. Buckley was a pill addict laid to rest a memory of the time when Buckley read me the riot act for writing about his godchildren in *Rolling Stone*. Titled "Life Without Father," the piece interviewed E. Howard Hunt's children Lisa and Saint John. It was the first behind-the-scenes piece published on Watergate. In it, the children spoke frankly of their painful dealings with their father. This was too close to the bone for William F. Buckley to bear. He phoned me at my parents' house over Christmas and gave me a real tongue-lashing. I countered by asking him exactly how close he really was to the children. Not very—I already knew the answer. Buckley sputtered in outrage that I dared to question him. It seems easy now to picture his icy demeanor being fed by a hand-ful of pills. The pills would support his conviction that he was king of the mountain.

Nigel is silent on the subject of William F. Buckley. Then he whispers that the pills are hearsay. But who better than an only child to know his parents' foibles?

The sky has finished with its hectic downpour. Little Charlotte has stopped shaking. Languid Tiger Lily sashays past my writing chair, out and about now that the storm has ended.

"Here, girl," I say, relieved to snap back to the pres-ent, leaving the Buckley family behind me. Outside my writing-room window, the twin towers of the El Dorado pierce a cobalt sky. More storms are predicted, but for the moment, we are in the clear.

What a relief: a sunny day with white, puffy clouds. Now it feels like summer. On her terrace, my friend Jennifer grows tomato plants: they are abundant, ripening on the vine. Yesterday marked a year since Jennifer's husband died. "Luther would have loved these," she says of her tomato plants.

"Luther would have" begins many of her sentences. She and her husband spent thirty years together. Even in death, they are together still. Friends are encouraging Jennifer to date. She is reluctant but open-minded. "There will never be another Luther," she says, and rightly so. Luther Davis wrote *Kismet* and *Grand Hotel*. He worked on dozens of films and kept on writing right up to his death at ninety-one. Since he died, Jennifer has overseen the careful transfer of his papers to the Smithsonian. She has given his movie script about Napoléon to a European producer, who has just e-mailed that he loves the script and wants to make a deal. He is interested, too, in a script Jennifer herself wrote. "That's Luther's doing, nudging along my career," Jennifer says.

It is true that in the year since Luther died, Jennifer has had a series of lucky breaks. She has a new agent, a new manager, and renewed work on *All My Children*, the soap opera she has worked on for more than thirty years. It is a heady mixture of the new and the old. Striving to take it all in, Jennifer misses the wise counsel of her husband. She talks to him when she is alone in their apartment. She listens to the quiet to try to hear his reply. "Luther is thrilled for me," she reports to her closest friends.

For those who knew them well as a couple, still in love as the decades passed, the possibility of an ongoing relationship seems very real. Jennifer has long entertained a strong belief in life after life. "I know he is still with me," she asserts with quiet urgency. She has consulted with two mediums, both of whom verify Luther's ongoing presence. "They say my career will be hopping," says Jennifer. "They say that Luther is on the case."

"You'll have to take some of these," Jennifer insists, indicating her summer crop of tomatoes. "You like fresh tomatoes, don't you?" she asks.

"Of course she does," I almost hear Luther answering for me.

"Of course I do," I answer.

Jennifer tells me the tale of scattering Luther's ashes. To do so, she made a special trip to California to share the anniversary of his death with his two daughters. The plan was to hike a canyon trail that Luther and Jennifer had loved to hike. At trail's end, the ashes would be scattered. That was the plan, but in executing it, Luther's daughters protested the steep grade. It was simply too dangerous to them, the shale-covered drop-off at canyon's end.

"What should I do?" Jennifer remembers praying, and, as if in answer, a bluebird flashed into view. (Luther loved birds.) Close behind it a flock of thirty birds swept out of a giant tree, Luther and Jennifer's favorite tree. As Jennifer and the girls watched, the birds banked sharply and wheeled back to perch again high in the branches of the tree. "Here, by the tree," Jennifer offered. "We used to hike to this tree."

Carefully, the three of them stepped down the slope to the tree's great trunk. The trunk held a hollow, a deep hole, that offered to be a chalice for Luther's ashes.

"We placed the ashes in the hole. Then we each said

what we needed to say," Jennifer recalls. Twittering birds in the tree's canopy joined in with the chorus of their voices. To Jennifer, their choir seemed to sing the song of Luther's soul.

"It was perfect," she exclaims, remembering. "Exactly perfect. First the solo bluebird and then the chorus of birds. We prayed to be guided, and we were."

"Nigel," I say, "you're the cause of my darkness and self-doubt." Nigel doesn't reply. He is not interested in shouldering any responsibility. I decide to outflank him by phoning an ally. I choose Sophy Burnham, one of the finest writers I know.

"Sophy? It's Julia. I am having a horrible time. I try to write and everything is coming out mangled."

Sophy listens to my complaint. "You sound exhausted,"

she says. "You sound like you need some time off and maybe a good, solid adventure."

"I'd love an adventure," I tell her. "In a month, I'm going up to Maine."

"You need an adventure now, not a month from now," she counters.

"That's true," I concur.

"Can you take your foot off the accelerator at least?"

"I have a deadline and I'm writing slowly. Not only that, I'm writing badly."

"Who told you that?" she asks.

"My Inner Censor. I call him Nigel."

"And for Nigel there's no doing it right?"

"Exactly."

"I suggest you call your publisher and lay your cards on the table. Maybe you can get an extension on your deadline. That would take some of the heat off, wouldn't it?"

"I guess it would, but I need to turn the book in on time so I'll have cash flow. I make my living off my writing.

I think if I stop writing for a while, I'll go crazy with financial anxiety."

Sophy listens sympathetically. "If it's too hard to do nothing, maybe you could try doing some research?" She names three titles she thinks may help. The third title is *Silences* by Tillie Olsen. It's a book I've read, respected, and disagreed with on writer's block.

"I can't afford any 'silences,'" I tell Sophy. "But I think I'll take you up on the suggestion I call my publisher. In fact, I happen to have a lunch scheduled with him for the day after tomorrow."

"You can get through till then?" Sophy asks, adding, "I'll call you that evening to hear how it went."

Just talking to Sophy has cut my sense of isolation and alienation in half. She knows exactly the writerly self-doubts I'm talking about. When I complain, she says, "Oh, yes." She has been there. She has grappled with her own Inner Censor, a character who gives Nigel a run for his money. I have heard Sophy's woes, those intervals when her writing is a crucifixion. To my ear, Sophy's doubts are nonsense. She has written many fine books and no poor ones. Her doubts are just self-flagellation, a price she pays for her very considerable gifts. Of course, to Sophy, my doubts are equal folly. She knows I will write further and well. But she hears my fears with an open heart, only pointing out that fear is an acronym for "False Evidence Appearing Real."

"Thanks for the ear," I say to Sophy.

"You're welcome. I've been where you are."

I feel a fluttering of hope. Sophy is writing and writing well. Maybe I, too, will recover.

It's not just a storm. It's a deluge. Water comes teeming down from the skies. My cab makes its way slowly. I am aimed for the Dog Ear Tavern, a publishing hangout. There I will meet my publisher, Joel Fotinos. I am nervous, determined to tell him the worst. I have tried four times to write him a book, and four times I've written poorly. I've hauled my most recent effort with me to prove my point.

Emma and I arrive at the restaurant before Joel. We are shown to a table near another larger table crowded with a boisterous, hard-drinking crowd.

"Can you hear?" I ask Emma.

"Barely," she answers.

"There he is!" Joel makes his way across the restaurant. He is wreathed in smiles, clearly glad to see us. He takes a chair.

"Can you hear?" I ask him.

"You get used to it, and the food's good," he answers. We settle in and catch up: news of the dogs; news of Joel's son, Rafael. Emma has pictures of Charlotte on her iPhone. Joel carries a laminated page of Rafael pictures. He looks darling, and Joel beams with fatherly pride. We place our lunch orders, and I give the conversation a decisive shove toward business.

"I've tried to write you a book four times now," I say. "None of them were any good."

Joel listens intently. He is not thrown by my tale of woe. "Maybe you need an extension on your deadline," he offers. "Maybe you should just take a breather."

Listening to Joel's suggestions, I feel a knot unknotting in my stomach. I am glad to have laid out my cards on the table. Joel is unflappable. His quiet strength is very reassuring.

"I'm afraid I've lost my voice," I tell him. "Here, let me show you what I mean."

With that, I haul my notebook out of my purse, open it to a random page, and begin reading. Somehow, magically, my prose seems stronger.

"I love it. Keep going," Joel interjects.

I flip through the pages to a particularly rotten passage. Reading it aloud, it suddenly sounds better.

"Read me some more," Joel interjects again.

I select another troublesome passage. I have in my head a litany of Nigel's judgments: the sentences are too short; the story is too personal; the chapter feels abbreviated; I'm practically writing shorthand . . . blah, blah, blah . . . Nigel's tone is derisive.

"I love it," Joel interrupts. "You know what you're doing, don't you?"

"No, what?" I answer weakly.

"You're writing a creative diary. You're letting us see up close and personal how you work your toolkit."

When Joel says the term "creative diary," I feel a weight slipping away from my psyche. A diary would use short sentences. A diary would contain abbreviated chapters. A diary would practically be written in shorthand. Instead of being a dismal failure, my pages are a success.

"I want you to disregard everything I said before," Joel announces. "Don't stop. Don't take an extension, just keep going: keep on doing exactly what you're doing. You've got a book on your hands."

I sit back in my chair. The conversation at the next table crests and then recedes as their meal is served. Outside the restaurant's plate-glass windows, the storm intensifies further still. I try to take in the ramifications of Joel's diagnosis: I have a book, possibly a good book, on my hands. Nigel nearly convinced me to abandon something good. For a moment, I have a sense of vertigo. I remember abandoning my first novel. Emily Hahn from *The New Yorker* had liked it and encouraged me. Instead of listening to her, I believed Nigel. The novel went into a desk drawer to live out its days. What other pieces of good work had Nigel sabotaged? I wrote and directed a feature film only to abandon it after a few festival appearances. Looking back, the film was good. Good in everyone's eyes but Nigel's. Now I have been writing forty-three years. Surely that should be long enough to have learned Nigel's tricks. But no. Nigel's tricks get trickier as the years wear on. I need the help of my friends to parry his attack. Joel is a friend indeed, daring to challenge Nigel's assertions.

"Thank you for listening," I say. I laugh aloud. Nigel is silenced.

"Oh, it was my pleasure," Joel replies. Our lunch is served. For once, I have a ravenous appetite.

The doorbell shrills and I open the door to a damp but cheerful Steven Fales, playwright and actor.

"Your hair! It looks wonderful! So youthful! So elegant!" He swoops me up in a bear hug. I kiss his cheek, leaving a crimson kiss. We settle onto a leather couch, giving each other a quick once-over. To my eye, Steven looks wonderful. He has just come back to New York after a grueling but satisfying run with his cabaret act, *Mormon American Princess*, in Provincetown, Massachusetts. He swapped his way through three venues, each one better than the last.

"I went to see ____." He names the friend of mine who is still in the hospital. "He couldn't talk, but we managed to have a lovely visit, reading lips."

"That's great."

"He had a sparkle in his eye. I thought, *Oh, good. He's going to make it.*"

"Yes, I think he is," I agree. It occurs to me that our friend must have mixed feelings about our visits. He doesn't want word to get out that he is ailing. He is in the midst of planning a one-man show, and a noted actor has expressed interest in playing him. Our friend would direct. It would be quite a coup if it all happened. There would be layer upon layer of artistry.

"I hope it all works out," says Steven. "There was an actor friend of his there at the same time. He is in a Broadway show right now."

Steven himself had a very successful off-Broadway show, *Confessions of a Mormon Boy.* Our ailing friend helped him to shape that show. Steven values him as a mentor.

"I have a present for you," I say, taking out a copy of *Prayers to the Great Creator*, a compilation of four prayer books I have written. "I feel a little strange giving you a prayer book, knowing you may have a whole collection of Mormon prayers."

"Oh, no," Steven says eagerly. "I'm open to any prayers. Mormons don't have set prayers."

"Well, then, good," I say. "These are the concepts that undergird *The Artist's Way*." I open the prayer book to a selection from *Blessings*. Steven avidly reads the prayer.

"I'm going to like having this," he says.

Conversation turns to Steven's career. His cabaret act went over very well in Provincetown. He hopes to shape it further. He is set to make a documentary of *Confessions of a Mormon Boy*, and he has a date slated for a reading of his third work, *Missionary Position*. He is writing daily, hard at work on a memoir.

"It all sounds wonderful," I tell him.

"It all feels good," he answers. Then he checks his watch and does a double take. "I'm due uptown," he apologizes.

"Let me get you a bag for your book," I offer.

"Thanks for the visit."

"Thank you for the visit." With another bear hug, he is out the door. He has an uptown meeting at four and then a pot-roast dinner party at seven. As I watch him walk to the elevator, I think he is a delightful mix of show business and apron strings.

Sunlight floods the apartment. The sky outside my writing room is blue with puffball clouds. I have a lunch appointment at the Popover Café with Emma and my literary agent, Susan Raihofer. There is just time enough to race through my Morning Pages, then it's off to the Popover, where I will abstain from the namesake treat. My lunch is salmon and salad. My treat is an iced cappuccino. The caffeine helps me to focus. Susan wants to know the details of my meeting with Joel. I tell her my good news: Joel loves the book so far.

"I want to see it," she says.

I explain that the book is in longhand and that it won't be suitable for viewing until I have it typed. "But he liked it," I conclude.

We talk next of the paperback publication of my novel *Mozart's Ghost*. We brainstorm over publicity ideas, ticking off venues for signings and radio shows that might welcome the book. We explore the use of Facebook and Twitter, two avenues for getting the word out. We decide we need to know more and be more proactive. It's time to become modern.

Their popovers arrive along with tiny vats of strawberry butter. Emma and Susan both slather their popovers with butter. Across the table from me, they look delectable but fattening. I sip at my cappuccino.

"Remember my short-story collection, *Popcorn*?" I ask Susan.

"I do," says Susan.

"I'm thinking we should try to get them published by a good New York publisher."

"*Mmm*," says Susan, cautiously interested.

"I think those stories were good and the press that published them went out of business as soon as they were off the press."

"I'd need you to update them by a story or two. I'd like a celebrity introduction, too."

Our salads arrive, and with them, a wave of optimism. If I am willing to do the work necessary for a fresh submission, the stories stand a chance of being picked up. I am daunted by Susan's list of requirements, but I can do it. All it takes is determination. My stories deserve a second chance at life. I owe it to them.

Susan picks at her salmon salad. She is too distracted by plotting a submission to focus on the more mundane chore of eating. In fact, she is skinny. Food for thought counts for more with her than actual food.

"What's going on with your musicals?" Susan asks. It's Emma's turn to take the floor.

"*The Medium at Large* has a director and a producer and an investor. All we need now is a venue," says Emma.

"Tell her about *Bunny's Bakery*," I urge Emma.

"It's a show I wrote myself," says Emma. "And we're getting wonderful feedback and lots of interest."

"That's wonderful," says Susan.

"Tell her about needing an agent on some sub-missions," I tell Emma.

"Yes, there are some places that require an agent to make the submission," says Emma shyly.

"I could do that for you," volunteers Susan.

"That's just wonderful," exclaims Emma. She picks at her tuna-melt sandwich, too excited to eat.

"Whatever I can do to help," Susan says.

"That's just wonderful," Emma repeats.

The waiter cruises past our table, eyeing our unfinished lunch. "Shall I pack these to go?" he asks Susan and Emma.

"That would be great," Susan answers.

"Yes, thank you," says Emma.

The waiter clears our plates and we sit for a moment quietly. There is the satisfaction of plans made. We get to our feet and kiss each other good-bye.

"Talk to you soon," I say.

"Talk to you soon," Susan echoes.

"Thank you," says Emma, thrilled to have the promise of forward motion. We say good-bye.

The walk home from the Popover is brief but eventful. Checking her iPhone, Emma finds a message from a friend. Her agent at William Morris has read *Bunny's Bakery*. She loves it, is very excited, and is brimming with ideas. Emma needs to give her a call.

"Oh my God!" exclaims Emma, stopping in her tracks.

"Give her a call," I coax. Emma stands rooted to the spot.

"I'd like to talk to my friend first," she says.

"So call her," I push, very excited at the news.

"I'll wait till we get home," says Emma. "Can you believe it?"

"I can believe it," I say. "The show is that good."

We lurch back into our walk.

Once at home, Emma calls her friend. She reiterates the good news. There's no mistake: the agent loves Emma's show. Prompted by me, Emma makes a call.

"Emma Lively? I was just about to call you," says the agent's assistant. "She wants to meet with you as soon as possible. Wednesday at three?"

"That would be fine," Emma says. "Wednesday at three." Off the phone, Emma pinches herself.

◦◦◦

At four o'clock Wednesday afternoon, my phone shrills. The squeaky voice on the other end of the line belongs to Emma. "She loves the show! She's going to represent it!"

"That's great, Emma!"

"She had all sorts of ideas."

"That's terrific!"

"What do we do now?"

"We celebrate. Let me take you to dinner."

We rendezvous with our friend Jane Cecil, an estimable actress.

"Goody," says Jane when we tell her Emma's news. "That's just wonderful." At eighty-three, Jane is a skilled recipient of news, good and bad. She is quietly gleeful at our good tidings. She saw the reading of *Bunny's Bakery* and had felt certain that good news would be in the offing.

"I can't believe it," Emma says.

"Learn to believe it," I counter.

"It's just such a shock," Jane says gently.

Emma and I catch a cab from Jane's up to a favorite restaurant, Sarabeth's. We ask to be seated at our favorite table. We don't need menus.

"I want mashed potatoes, spinach, and onion rings," Emma announces to our waiter.

"I'll have the crabcake appetizer with spinach," I put in. "And an iced cappuccino."

"I totally trust her. I felt like I just acted like myself in the meeting," Emma volunteers.

"I'm sure you were perfect," I say.

"I said Tyler and I played together like two seven-year-olds," she continues.

"That's fine," I say. "And you do."

"Maybe something good is about to happen," she says.

"Something good already did happen," I correct her. "She loves the show. Get used to it."

The plan is a one-o' clock lunch with my friend and student, an actor who is working on his memoir. We are meeting at a hole-in-the-wall restaurant at Fifteenth Street and Eighth Avenue. The menu is Cuban. The atmosphere homey. Emma and I arrive at one sharp. Entering the restaurant, we nab a table for four. When the waiter arrives, we explain we're meeting a friend. Fifteen minutes pass with no sign of our lunch date. We order iced coffee, plantains, and an avocado salad. At one twenty we get a text message from him: "Running late. More like one thirty." We order a second round of iced coffee and look around the restaurant. Its clientele is a schizophrenic mix of overweight diners and bodybuilders. Our waiter looks caught between the two. He's hefty, with bare muscular arms. He fusses over us a little, sympathetic that we are being stood up. When our friend finally arrives at two, our waiter is relieved for us. Our friend places our orders in rapid-fire Spanish. The waiter smiles. Clearly we have ordered well.

"So what's new?" he asks us. We tell him the news of Emma's new representation at William Morris. He's delighted for her. "Now you're free to focus on making things." He cuts to the chase.

"Yes, I can hardly believe it," says Emma.

"And what about you?" he asks me.

"I'm writing," I tell him.

"I've brought you a play I'm writing and a big cup from my narrative timeline."

"What's the cup?"

"It's a heavy one, my breakdown."

"It may take me a while to get these things read," I warn him.

"Take your time," he answers, handing me a thick folder of pages.

I remember that he is a good writer, and I tell myself that reading his work will be a treat, not a chore.

The waiter offers us dessert, but we settle for another round of iced coffee. "You know, I put off writing," he says. "Then I read your memoir and thought, *If she can do it, I can do it.*"

"I think that's a compliment," I say, signaling for the check.

"Of course it is," says Emma. We settle the check and kiss him good-bye.

The cab ride from the restaurant up to Mount Sinai Medi-cal Center takes twenty minutes and twenty dollars. We are determined to visit our ailing friend, but when we check in at reception, we learn that he has changed rooms and his new room is empty.

"He's just gone to physical therapy," volunteers a helpful nurse. "Go left to the end of the hall and you'll find him."

"We can go in there?" Emma asks.

"Go on. Go on," replies the nurse.

And so we go left to the end of the hall and we enter the wide double doors to physical therapy. It is a large room filled with exercise equipment. At the far end, we spot our friend. He is connected to an oxygen tank, and tubes seem to sprout from everywhere on his body. Nonetheless, he smiles widely when he spots us.

"Are we allowed to kiss you now?" we ask.

"Yes, yes," our friend mouths the permission. He still cannot speak, but Emma is very adept at reading his lips.

"He says yes," announces Emma, bending close to kiss his cheek.

"I'm Diane," the physical therapist introduces herself. "Are you family?"

"We're friends," I say.

"Good friends," puts in Emma.

"Good friends," mouths our friend.

Diane sets to work, attaching weights to our friend's arms. "I want you to raise your arm fifteen times," she instructs. "Can you do that?" Obediently, our friend sets to work, counting one to fifteen, raising and then lowering his right arm.

"Good," says Diane. "Now let's try the other side." She attaches the weight to his left arm. "Fifteen times," she says, and our friend again sets to work but with more difficulty. His left side is weaker. When he finally reaches fifteen, Diane is quick to praise him. "That's very good," she announces. Our friend makes a wry little shrug.

"We've got hot news," I tell him. "Emma has been taken on by an agent at William Morris."

"Wonderful!"

Diane rotates his arm out to the side, flapping it like a wing. "Fifteen times," she instructs. Our friend flaps his arm up and down.

"Like a chicken," he jokes. Emma reads his lips and laughs at his joke. We step to one side to give him room to flap his left arm.

"Very good," pronounces Diane. Our friend smiles.

"We'd better be going," I announce, feeling we are deflecting our friend's attention. "We'll come back soon. Lots of love."

"Lots of love," Emma echoes. We retrace our steps back to the wide double doors, then down the corridor to the exit.

"He's much better," I say with relief.

"Yes," says Emma. "I think he is."

It's late in the day to start writing. I consider waiting until tomorrow, and then I think, *No. I'll grab a few sentences.* Over the years, I have learned to grab tidbits of time. The tidbits add up. It is an "easy does it" approach to creativ-ity. Small tidbits add up to a larger whole.

Telling myself I need to read only a little of my friend's memoir, I dip a toe in. One page leads to another. Page builds upon page, and in no time I have whisked through all he has given me. He is a sharp and vivid writer. All his actor's tricks of sense memory serve him very well. His narrative is crammed with telling details. The reader is with him every step of the way as he walks down memory lane. There it is on the page: his life as a young, headstrong actor—the heady success, the misplaced arrogance, the crippling breakdown that swept in on him from nowhere. There are sleepless nights, bursts of manic energy, bouts of deadly depression. It is all laid out without apology. Events speak for themselves.

I call him and he is surprised to hear from me so soon. I have no criticism of his pages but one: I want more. I feel he can provide even more details of the breakdown he had while playing a Broadway lead.

"Yes, I can do that," he answers gamely.

Reading my friend's pages, I am struck by his courage. I suffer from breakdowns, but they have been largely private. His demons share the stage with him. He has wrestled with them in public—wrestled and won. Without his pages to tutor me, I would never have guessed his battles.

It took twenty years to get a correct diagnosis. It took five more years of tinkering with medicines. "Chemical imbalance" is a literal term. Doctors try a little of this and a little of that to make the scales come out even. Finally, they are balanced and my friend has been restored to his sunny self.

"I know it's difficult, revisiting such a hard time."

"I can do it. It's actually healing to remember and get it on the page."

"Well, then. I'll wait for more pages."

"You got it," he says brusquely.

We get off the phone.

I am set to address an award-winning group of high school writers. They have been doing Morning Pages and want to hear more about them straight from the horse's mouth. I get out a copy of my book *The Right to Write*, and I thumb through it, seeking out topics for my talk. It occurs to me that I should teach them the basic tools from *The Artist's Way*. If they do Morning Pages, Artist's Dates, and walks, they should develop some stable grounding as writers. They are all around eighteen. I was that age when I committed to writing. They are not too young to make a similar commitment.

I want to tell them that they don't need anyone's permission to be a writer. I want to tell them to trust, that the universe has a plan for them and their work. I want to tell them to ignore the odds stacked against them and to believe they can have a vocation despite the odds. I want to tell them that they can count on synchronicity, that they will experience lucky breaks. I will talk to them about the need to simply write, quoting from the film *Field of Dreams*, "Build it and they will come." Eighteen is not too young to begin following their own stars. Writing is a matter of faith, I want to tell them. A habit of faith will stand them in good stead. If this sounds too woo-woo, I need to tell them that it is nonetheless my writer's experience. I will urge them to experiment and record the results.

At Random House, the guard at the security desk directs me to the second floor, where the elevator opens to a large poster-board sign announcing "The Summer Writers' Conference." I wind my way through a maze of offices to a balcony housing a large wooden table and seating for the young writers, who look younger than young. My host, Richard Hoehler, has cued the young writers to select a passage of their work to be read. I am introduced and then we go around the table, with each writer reading a few paragraphs. The selections are dramatic. Clearly the writers have that necessary ingredient: imagination.

At Richard's cue, I begin talking, hoping to be able to reach the writers despite the forty-odd years yawning between us. I teach them Morning Pages, which they have already been practicing. They are alert and receptive. Next I launch into Artist Dates, and here I have to tap-dance to keep their attention. I explain that writing uses images and that Artist Dates restock our inner image pond. Third, I explain the power of walking, the way it works to integrate our insights and inspirations. When I finish talking, I ask for questions, and to my dismay there are none. We sit in uncomfortable silence until one young writer musters her nerve to ask a question about discouragement. I answer her carefully, citing the importance of finding Believing Mirrors, those people who believe in us and our potential. I urge the writers to stay in touch with one another. To my delight, Richard has a stack of contact sheets at the ready. After another pregnant pause, a writer asks about the danger of being a dilettante. There is no danger, I tell her. We need to write what seems to want to be written. A writing career is not linear, I tell her. The idea that it should be or can be is just a need to control. Heads nod around the table. They've already had the experience of trying to be controlled.

The clock strikes three. My time with the young writers is over. They gather together their papers and notebooks. Richard passes out the contact sheets. A Random House editor suggests that they pose for a group picture. *How corny*, you can practically hear them thinking even as they line up, clustered around the sign announcing the conference.

"A little closer together, please," the editor implores. Obligingly, the writers cluster closer.

"That's great," announces the editor, squeezing off a few shots. "I'll get these out to you." The writers disperse, making their way to the elevator. I am hoping that they carry with them a more firmly forged identity as writers.

It is a hot, humid, and cloudy afternoon. A thunderstorm is expected momentarily, which should cool things down. More than one hundred trees were uprooted in Central Park by our last thunderstorm. Winds up to eighty miles per hour struck savagely. For once the dogs' apprehension was well founded. Just now, Charlotte and Tiger Lily are stretched out napping. It is so hot they don't want to go outside. Charlotte dozes with one ear cocked to hear the grinding of the elevator. Emma has been gone, in Chicago for nine days, and Charlotte keeps hoping that the elevator signals her arrival home. Tiger Lily, too, misses her, as do I. She is due back tomorrow, and not a moment too soon.

For a week and a half, I have lived alone, walking the dogs three times daily. When Emma announced her plan to go to Chicago, I did a quick mental tally. Ten days times three dog walks equals thirty dog walks. I was daunted at the prospect, but I also knew that one day at a time, one walk at a time, it could be done. Now we are in the home stretch, one day and a half, five dog walks, until Emma is home.

Emma went to Chicago to spend a week's "vacation" inspecting theaters, meeting artistic directors, and spending time with our newfound collaborators. She has also spent a good deal of time with Tyler. Like Emma, Tyler is eager to forge ahead. Like her, he chomps at the bit. "Just do it" is his motto and ours.

Now the clouds are darkening and thunder rumbles in the distance. Charlotte is nervously barking, trembling with dread. Tiger Lily is still as a stone, her usual strategy for outwitting the storm. When I talked to Emma last, she sounded ready to come home. Her progress report was sunny optimism, clouded by fatigue.

"I have so much to tell you!" she exclaims during a late-night phone call.

"We all miss you," I assure her. "The dogs go to the door every time the elevator comes to our floor. I keep telling them, 'Soon.'"

"I'm almost home," Emma says. We get off the phone eager to catch up in person. I take the dogs out for their evening walk.

The phone shrills. I pick it up. It is Emma, phoning home to announce her flight has been canceled. The next available flight is at six a.m. tomorrow morning. She will stay with Tyler, sleeping a little before going to the airport to catch her plane.

"Have fun," I urge her.

"We're actually so excited to have one more day," she answers.

And so I resign myself to two extra dog walks.

"She'll be home tomorrow," I tell Charlotte. We will have twenty-four hours before setting out to Maine. It is time for our yearly vacation, a two-week hiatus spent with Emma's family. They live in central Maine on a pristine lake where we go swimming, kayaking, and canoeing. The sky by night is a star-spangled glory. As night falls, the loons set up their ghostly calls. Emma can do a creditable imitation.

When Emma arrives home, she is exhausted. "I think I should go to bed," she announces. She retreats to her wing of the apartment with Charlotte at her heels. She is half asleep.

I set about packing for Maine. Experience has tutored me to expect chilly nights. I pack two warm jackets and flannel pajamas. I pack a separate bag of books and writing supplies. I bring my Morning Pages journal, and two other journals for my current projects. As I discussed with Susan, my agent, I am working on my short-story collection, *Popcorn*. I want to update it, possibly add new stories. It will be my bedtime reading on the trip: that, and my prayer book *Answered Prayers*.

When Emma wakes she says, "I don't think that red-eye flights are a very good idea for me. Do you want to drive to Maine right now?"

"No," I tell her. "I don't think it's good to do long hours of nighttime driving. Let's leave early in the morning."

"OK," Emma reluctantly agrees, but she packs her bag and announces, "I'm ready to go now."

"No," I insist. "We'll travel when it's light."

"Oh, all right," says Emma. "But I'm getting up at six so that we can be on the road by eight."

We are on the road by eight. The dogs settle into the back-seat on two sheepskin throws. Emma cues up *Bunny's Bakery* on the stereo. It is great driving music, very upbeat. We make our way north, out of the city, stopping once we are in Connecticut for gasoline and coffee.

Back on the road, we cue up *The Medium at Large*. This demo is a little less polished than *Bunny's Bakery* but enjoyable nonetheless. As rain clouds begin to spatter us, we get current with each other. I tell Emma about life in New York without her, and she tells me about her Chicago adventures. We are glad to see each other and we are each glad that we were missed. To my ear, Emma's Chicago trip sounds hectic but rewarding. We are both invited back, mid-September. We hope to have a firm plan by then.

As we make our way north, a tropical storm chases us up the coast. Trying to outrun it, we do not stop for a meal. When we reach the narrow two-lane highway north of Portland, the storm catches us. We drive the final thirty miles in a deluge, wipers frantically beating. Finally, we make the turn into Wilton, feeling like we are in a submarine, so intense is the rain. At Emma's parents' house, we pilot the car up the steep hill. Turning into their drive, we pull up under a large maple tree. The tree is scant shelter from the storm.

"I'm going to make a run for it," Emma decides.

"I'm going to wait it out," I counter.

Emma dashes for the house. I stay behind in the car. A few minutes later, Emma's father looms into view carrying a large umbrella. Together, we ferry the dogs up the hill into the house. The umbrella keeps us dry—sort of.

My bedroom is tucked up high beneath the eaves. It features lace curtains and floral-sprigged wallpaper. The bed is a cherrywood four-poster. The sheets are floral and flannel. Two quilts and a soft pink blanket complete the warmth. My first night in Maine, I fall asleep immediately, sleeping the clock round. Breakfast is a bowl of freshly picked blueberries topped by cottage cheese or yogurt. After that, it's time for a trip over to the Lake House.

Emma's parents have two houses, the snug bungalow in which we stay and a lakeside condominium perched on the shore of Wilson Lake. The condominium is dubbed the Lake House, and it features kayaking and canoeing. At night on the lake, the loons make their haunting calls and a great blue heron swoops down to roost. An eagle lands on the small island just off shore. The Lake House is a birder's paradise.

In a week, Emma will host Tyler on his first visit to Maine. They are working on a new show called *The Blue*

Lobster. There actually is such a thing as a blue lobster, a one-in-two-million occurrence. In the week before Tyler's arrival, Emma will go lobster fishing on remote Swan's Island.

We set out to experience the Maine woods. Rob Lively, Emma's father, goes kayaking on the far reaches of Wilson Lake. He spots a moose track "the size of a dinner plate." And a smaller deer track as well. The eagle pays a visit. It's too bad Tyler is not yet in residence. The flora and fauna of Maine are showing off.

For me, the high point of the day is my visit to Kineo-watha Park. God lives in the park, I am convinced. The white pines there tower well over a hundred feet. There is a lib-eral scattering of pinecones. Rob explains that in season, the great white pines give off a fine yellow dust—pollen. It is not the season now, so the pinecones lie on bare ground. I scoop a couple of magnificent specimens. On the way back to the house, I gather goldenrod, clover, and sweet-smelling Queen Anne's lace. Rob kids me that I am building an altar—and I am. The mere sight of the humble bouquet fills me with joy.

For five years now I have pilgrimaged to Maine in August. Blueberry season is in full swing. Strawberries are done already. I lie on the ground under the blueberry bushes. The berries fall at the touch. They seem bigger this year. All of Maine seems lovelier. Still not so beautiful as my beloved Taos but beautiful enough. The goldenrod vies with chamisa. The white pines challenge the cottonwoods. The Queen Anne's lace has a perfume, nearly as heady as sage. Each year longer that I am away from Taos, Maine casts its spell. The lakes vie with the mountains and may one day win out. Maybe next year.

Home in New York, I settle in to my familiar routine, writing daily, walking the dogs, reading. Emma is set to go back to Maine for the weekend, this time with Tyler in tow. She has gone to pick him up at the airport. Charlotte senses their arrival before the key turns in the lock, running to the door with a toy, "ratty," to offer them. I get up to greet them as they enter the apartment. They are chattering with excitement. Remarkably, not one but two blue lobsters were caught on Swan's Island.

"They're auditioning for the show." Emma laughs.

Tyler lights up as he sees me, hugging me tightly. "You're wasting away!" he exclaims.

"Your voice to God's ear," I reply. He spent the summer watching me eat chopped salads and cucumber-yogurt soup, attempting to be a picture of health while he and Emma maintained an obnoxious but delectable-looking diet of macaroni and cheese, candy, and pizza.

"So you're off to Maine in the morning. Are you going to eat a lobster?" I ask Tyler.

The answer? "Absolutely." A Midwesterner by birth and rearing, Tyler has never been to Maine, and with *The Blue Lobster* set there, he needs some firsthand experience. Emma is hell-bent on taking him to a lobster shack as soon as they arrive.

"We have to take you to a lighthouse, too," she insists.

"Maybe our main character lives in the lighthouse!" Tyler suggests.

The next morning they are off, and in the evening, they call to report in: coleslaw, corn on the cob, and lobster—a real Maine hoedown. ("A giant orange bug but delicious," pronounces Tyler.) Conversation with a lobsterman—the real Maine lowdown. A day at the shore and an evening at the Lake House, where they stayed out in the paddleboat past sunset. Breakfast tomorrow will feature blueberry pancakes.

I hang up the phone and take the dogs for their evening walk. I picture Emma and Tyler settling in for the night, accompanied by the haunting cries of the loons. When Tyler leaves, he will be sorely missed. "He's your Muse," I tell Emma, "and you're his."

At nine fifteen, the line for admission to the nine forty-five show was already formed. Mary, the hostess, sweet-talks the crowd into compliance. We are here to see my friend Steven's one-man show, *Mormon American Princess*. The crowd is varied, as much heterosexual as not, from twenties to sixties, some dapper, some not.

Steven Fales put himself on the map with *Confessions of a Mormon Boy*, his first one-man show, directed by the legend Jack Hofsiss. In that show, Steven threaded a tale from Mormon boyhood to youthful marriage to various therapies intended to cure him of homosexual urges. The therapies failed. Steven was irretrievably gay. He was excommunicated by the church, then launched into a self-destructive spiral of drink, drugs, and sex. Desperate, he turned to writing. The writing led him back to sanity. Restored to his dignity, he offered his show as a cautionary tale. The new show, *Mormon American Princess*, is a coming-out story. Good humor replaces pathos.

At nine forty-five, the crowd is still filing in. I am here with Emma; my daughter, Domenica; and her boyfriend. We are given a booth, elevated at center stage. We order round one of our obligatory two rounds of drinks. I sip at an orange juice on the rocks. At nine fifty-five, a hush falls over the room. "There he is," someone breathes. All eyes are riveted on Steven, clad in blue jeans, cowboy boots, and a leather shirt. He looks like the Westerner that he is. For his opening number he does some musical gender-bending. He belts and then croons his way through "Son of a Preacher Man." Steven has an incandescent sexuality that floods the stage. When he talks about sexual desire, the audience can feel it. Oddly, Steven's sexual charisma throws a monkey wrench into his show. The show tilts to accommodate the audience's lust.

Midway through his act, Steven performs another gender-bender. He sings, "I Don't Know How to Love Him," Mary Magdalene's showstopper from *Jesus Christ Superstar*. The song reflects a promiscuous past—Steven's as well as Magdalene's. Part confessional, part sheer entertainment, the evening is uneven but engrossing. What clearly emerges is a sense of his impressive talent.

His audience responds with bursts of applause, and at show's end a sustained round of enthusiasm. Steven is pleased by the show's reception. The evening was his debut back in New York, and it made him feel there was a place for him and his work.

"Thanks for coming out," Steven stops by to tell our table.

"Thank *you*," we respond.

"Mom, I am thinking of getting some kelly green shoes," Domenica phones to tell me. "They have little snaffle bits and a one-inch heel. What do you think?"

"They sound darling," I tell her. Two hours later we meet for dinner, and she is wearing the shoes and they are darling.

"Let's get some grilled calamari," I suggest, looking over the menu. We are at Elephant & Castle, a favored haunt, under the careful gaze of Tony, our favorite waiter. "I'll have an iced cappuccino," I tell him. Domenica opts for peppermint tea.

It is a Wednesday, the day we regularly meet at Elephant & Castle. Domenica has a lot on her plate, and I am eager to hear the details. She is set to teach a filmmaking seminar in Kentucky. She is set to direct a short. I want news of all of it.

In Kentucky, she will be co-teaching with an actress named Veronica. Veronica just canceled plans to get together in New York. Domenica worries about their going out there unrehearsed. She has received a multipage e-mail detailing the hosts' expectations. It sounds daunting.

The short she will be directing is written by noted playwright Richard Nelson. It is a sort of calling card for Domenica's work. She is set to direct a feature by Nelson later in the year. The short is fourteen pages of dialogue. She will have three days to shoot it. She will be traveling to Maine on location.

Domenica orders a smoked mozzarella salad. I order bacon, pear, and endive. As we settle in to eat, I reflect that it's thirty years since Domenica and I first explored this block. We lived here in the West Village when she was a toddler. She attended P.S. 41, just up the street. We would "ride" there on her stick horse. And now, today, she wears "horsey" shoes. Some tastes do not change.

Domenica asks if she can borrow my car for the shoot. I'm delighted to loan it to her. It is a Honda CR-V with four-wheel drive—ideal for the trip to Maine. Domenica is a careful driver, but I want her to have the extra safety of my car. Perhaps because we are in her childhood neighborhood, I catch myself feeling extra protective. When our calamari arrive at the table, I marvel to myself that Domenica likes such grown-up food.

"But, Mom—I am a grown-up!" Domenica exclaims.

I'm still in bed, but the apartment is flooded with music. Emma is at the keys trying out a melody for *The Blue Lobster*. The show opens on the coast of Maine as the sun rises. Emma's music begins at night, then shifts to sunrise. By song's end, it is full daylight. The sun sparkles on the Atlantic. Emma's piano sparkles as well, rippling like waves.

"It sounds great, Emma," I call out.

"I didn't mean to wake you," Emma responds.

"That's OK. It's great," I tell her.

"You think so?"

"Yes, really."

"Listen to this. The animals waking up." Theme by theme, Emma introduces the great blue heron, the cormorants, the seagulls, the seal, and then the starfish, the puffin, and last the rare blue lobster.

"You don't think it's bad starting at sunrise? I mean, *The Lion King* opens at sunup."

"So did *Oklahoma!*" I reassure her. "Nobody accused *The Lion King* of copycatting."

Emma launches into a new melody, this time a melancholy one. It is moody and very beautiful.

"What's that?" I call out when she has finished.

"It's when the friends are separated," Emma answers. "They miss each other. Can you hear that?"

"Yes, yes, I can," I say. I am now thoroughly awake, and I pad into the living room.

Tiger Lily and Charlotte are mesmerized by the music. They lie beneath the piano, heads nearly on the pedals. Emma tries out yet another new melody. This one is comic, a blues number for Mama Lobster. Emma belts out the lyric:

> I got a hundred thousand kids that wanna be fed,
> I got seventy thousand still wettin' the bed.
> And if I'm only ever s'posed to procreate,
> How'm I ever s'posed to gonna lose this weight?
> Oh, I'm stressed, I'm stressed, I'm stressed.

Wrapping up the tune, Emma explains, "Lobsters really do have hundreds of thousands of babies, and 'breeder' lobsters cannot be caught in Maine—so Mama Lobster really would just keep getting bigger and bigger. Tyler and I are trying to be really true to nature with this show."

"But also funny?" I ask.

"We sure hope so!"

It is a clear, cool, and crisp autumn day. Emma has gone to Indianapolis to visit her college roommate, Pam French. Once more I am left in charge of the dogs, who trail after me from room to room. Without Emma, the house is quiet. I have grown spoiled, accustomed to her good nature, accustomed, too, to her music. Tomorrow I have scheduled a piano lesson with my wise and delightful teacher Chaim Freiberg. I am resuming lessons after a lapse of six months. I am resuming them because I found myself saying, "Emma is the real musician."

In other words, I was becoming a shadow artist,

someone who lived in the shadow of a declared artist. I could barely remember the days and years when I went to the piano eagerly, picking out new melodies. I barely remember that I wrote melodies. I have slipped back into thinking of myself as nonmusical, the definition of myself I was raised with. Officially the "nonmusical" member of a large and talented musical family. I was forty-five before I began writing music. How happy it made me to find melodies. But now I have lost them again.

With Emma gone, the piano stands abandoned. Its silent keys beckon to me. There's no one here to judge my halting playing; no one to judge my melodies. Tomorrow's lesson will focus on me as a musician, but I might take to the keys tonight.

Emma doesn't try to intimidate me. In fact, she is generous in her praise of my fledgling musicianship.

"I like that, Julie," she may call to me as I pick out a new melody.

"Thank you," I call back, thrilled by her enthusiasm, daunted that she is listening. I first began writing music in

London, an ocean away from my family's critical ears. No one in London knew me, knew whether I was musical or not. Alone in a rented flat, I felt free enough to try writing music. With no one to critique my melodies, they came to me easily and often.

Over the course of a summer, I wrote my musical *Avalon*. Using an alphabetical code to take my melodies down, I approximated musical notation. Singing my songs into a tape recorder, I safeguarded my melodies from being lost or forgotten. When Emma entered my world, she transformed my alphabetical code into bona fide musical notation. Trained by her long years as a violist to hear harmony, she harmonized my melodies. With Emma's help, my melodies became "real." We entered a happy period of several years when I wrote music daily and Emma rushed along close afterward, supplying harmony.

"I can't write melody," Emma believed at the time. But then I got sick—in fact, I was hospitalized—and left to her own devices, Emma began hearing melodies. Judy Collins, my friend, stepped in to be Emma's mentor.

"Write ninety songs in ninety days," Judy advised her. "Write about anything and everything, be it a color, or somebody's name, or whatever mood you are in—just write."

Egged on by Judy's enthusiasm, Emma did write ninety songs in ninety days. "I was transformed," she recalls. "At the end of ninety days, I was a songwriter."

So now Emma is a songwriter. She prefers that word to *composer*. The piano doesn't care what she calls herself. It rings out gladly at her touch. And it will ring out gladly at mine. I open the folder that contains Chaim's handwritten music. I am delighted to find I can still pick out his beautiful melodies.

It's a gray and rainy day, not a deluge, just a light, constant drizzle. I flag a cab and give the address of Saint Bartholomew's Church at Fifty-first Street and Park Avenue. I am en route to see a reading of Steven's new play, *Missionary Position*, which details his two years as a Mormon missionary in Portugal. Not yet at peace with his homosexuality, Steven spent his missionary years yearning—yearning for sex, yearning for connection, yearning for acceptance.

As Steven reads his adventures, his audience, mainly gay Episcopalians, is with him. There are rueful laughs and collective sighs. By journey's end, the audience is won over completely. Steven's long road to self-acceptance is one many of them have traveled. Several years after being excommunicated from the Mormon Church, he joined Episcopalianism. His new church received him with open arms. Saint Bart's, as it's affectionately called, offered Steven a reading with a buffet lunch ahead of time and coffee and dessert afterward. His reading is held in the Terrace Room, a handsome, wood-paneled room that seats a hundred. Most of the chairs are filled.

Steven does an uncanny job of capturing the universal struggles of adolescence. Who as an adolescent hasn't suffered from an unrequited love? Mine was over a boy named

Bob O'Leary. Early this year I got an e-mail from Lynne Burke, the girl he married instead. Did I remember her? she wondered. For my part, how could I forget? Listening to Steven's recollections, I wince at their poignancy. I join the crowd in prolonged applause as Steven's show draws to a close.

Now the rain is a steady downpour. Emma and I hide under a black umbrella. We flag down a cab and give the address of a club called the Blue Note. We are bound to see a singer named Judith Owen. Owen has a devoted following. Emma has seen her perform before and is eager for me to hear her.

The Blue Note is a long, narrow club with a small raised stage mid-room. Owen is playing two sets, at eight and ten thirty. We are early for the eight-o'clock. The

Playbill waxes rapturous about Owen's talents. She is a charmer and a seducer, a rocker and a jazz chanteuse. A musician's musician. The room is filled to capacity. Eager chat flows from table to table.

"Ladies and gentlemen, Judith Owen," booms the speaker system, and Owen, clad in black slacks and shirt and a silver jacket, steps onstage. She has long red hair and a soulful spirit. She launches into a blues ballad. The room quiets down to serious listening.

Her set is an eclectic mix of blues, pop, jazz, and some classic covers, most notably "Night and Day." Her audience calls out requests for favorites. Owen obliges them. As the evening wears on, her rapport with her audience deepens. It is clear that many of her followers do, in fact, follow her from gig to gig. At set's end, Owen stands outside her dressing room autographing CDs. The line for her signature snakes nearly out the door.

Owen is a good sport about meeting with her audience. They clearly identify with her, and she with them. Signing takes nearly an hour. Finally, she retreats to her dressing room for a scant half-hour's break, inviting us in to visit.

"This is quite a crowd for a Monday night," she exclaims, clearly pleased. "I wasn't expecting such a turn-out," she says modestly.

The crowd for the second show is even larger than the first. Judith is eager to perform for them. She enjoys her audience's enthusiasm, and is not at all aloof or absorbed by her own celebrity. At the cue, "Ladies and gentlemen, Judith Owen," she steps gladly to the stage.

The evening is chill. It feels like November, not September. I flag a cab and settle in for the ride down to the West Village. I am meeting Domenica for an early supper and then heading to the Open Center to teach week two of a twelve-week Artist's Way class. As always when I teach, I am nervous.

Domenica is waiting for me at Elephant & Castle. She wears a brown angora sweater that matches her hair and eyes. She looks a little beat, and then I remember why: she traveled to Louisville to teach a seminar over the weekend.

"So how'd it go?" I ask her.

"I'm glad it's over," she replies.

"And?" I press.

"And it went well, I think," she answers. We order iced cappuccinos and large salads. She fills me in on her teaching adventure. It was tricky—half of the class were nervous newcomers; half of the class were quite experienced. Add to this the fact that Domenica was co-teaching with an actress who wanted to stress different points than she did. "I was lucky to get out with my skin," Domenica concludes.

"I'm sure you did better than that," I counter.

"Well, maybe," she replies. She used Affirmations and Blurts, an *Artist's Way* tool, and it worked very well, she adds. Her class then had an even playing field. She brightens, talking about the experience. I brighten, too, picturing her at work. I have seen Domenica speak in public before and know her to be poised and graceful.

"So stick me in the prayer pot for tonight," I put in just as our salads arrive.

"How do you like this bunch of students?" Domenica asks.

"I think they have a good sense of humor," I answer.

"That's nice," says Domenica.

"Yes. That's very nice," I say.

Our salads are delicious and take our full focus for a while.

We finish our salads and Domenica orders blueberry crumb pie for dessert. I keep one eye on the clock, wanting to arrive at the center early.

"Time to go?" Domenica asks.

"Yes, I'm afraid so," I answer.

The cab ride to Thirtieth Street and Madison Avenue is brief. The Open Center has moved from its home in SoHo to a new venue near Madison Square Park. I find myself resenting the new location. I enjoyed the hipness factor of teaching in SoHo. The new building is more spacious, and its teaching rooms are luxurious. Still, I prefer the old.

At the center, I am ushered to a small office on the third floor. Emma meets me there. She always accompanies me when I teach—she sets up the teaching and double-checks the venue. During class, she is an anchor and a calming presence. I have half an hour to review my teaching notes and see if I have any additions or corrections to make. Sandy Levine, the program director, drops by to check on me. An aide comes by to take a Starbucks order. I ask for a Venti peppermint tea. No sooner does the tea arrive than it is time to go down a floor to my classroom. It's still ten minutes before class, but I like to get there early and put my teaching notes up on a flip chart.

My planned agenda is a rigorous one, and I'm hoping the class is up to it. They are skeptical, and have a "show me, prove it to me" attitude. They want me to explain everything in intellectual terms. I know from experience that they are far better off simply *doing*. And so, unpopular but determined, I start with the exercise called U-turns (I teach this tool to every class, just at differing weeks according to their degree of readiness). The task asks students to trace the times they have quit an art form and why. It is a deepwater exercise surfacing a lot of grief and shame. Typically U-turns are a source of self-flagellation. Just getting them out in the open is tremendously healing. But the procedure is volatile, so I am braced for the possibility of a class rebellion. A category at a time, I tick off potential U-turns.

"Did you ever do a U-turn around writing?" I ask. "Or music? Or visual arts? Did you ever do a U-turn regarding theater? Or film? Or crafts?"

Each question moves the class deeper into self-inventory. A hush falls over the room. Now I break the class into clusters of three and have them go, one category at a time, sharing their U-turns. At the start, voices are hushed and solemn. As they progress, there is a ripple of laughter. Clusters grow louder. Confessions come more

freely. By the time they reach the last category, the clusters are bubbling over. They have ventilated a great deal of
toxic shame. I congratulate them on their courage.

In the cab on the way home, I say to Emma, "I'm glad
that tool is over with. I think they did very well."

"You did well, too," Emma says. "I know you were
nervous, but it didn't show."

"This class may be too smart for their own good. They
would rather have an explanation than an experience. My job
is to get them into the water, but they are resistant. Did you
notice their body language? Folded arms and tilted heads—
but they relaxed as the categories unfolded. I just hope every
week isn't going to be an exercise in skepticism."

I am scheduled to have a piano lesson every Saturday at
two p.m. Chaim is infinitely patient with my tortoise-paced

progress. I look forward to my lesson and play through the pieces several times. Our repertoire is largely wonderful songs that Chaim has written. He has a beautiful, mournful sense of melody. I love the pieces we play.

Chaim arrives—doffing his leather jacket and his backpack. He has stopped at Starbucks and arrives carrying a Venti coffee, which we will split. We sit at the window, watching the rain. It is still coming down.

"I'm ready," I say, setting aside my coffee mug. Chaim follows suit, and we settle in at the piano. I have practiced and can play most of our pieces smoothly. We play "Lullaby," "Autumn Song," and "Old Castle." After I play each piece, I ask Chaim to play it through so I can hear what it truly sounds like. He plays them all, however simple, with passion and conviction. His past as a concert pianist shows in his playing.

Midway through the lesson we tackle something Chaim didn't write. It is a Russian song called "The Beautiful Bride." Spanning two octaves, it is tricky to play. I ask Chaim to play it once through. Like so many of the pieces we play, it is sad and beautiful. I try to capture the spirit of the piece but find I am still focused on just getting the notes right. I remind myself I am taking lessons to learn. Still, it's hard not to judge myself in comparison to my brother Christopher, to my friend Bob McDonald, and, despite his kindness, to Chaim.

As if sensing my discontent, Chaim gives a final melancholy ripple to the keys.

"Maybe that's enough for today," he says.

I remind him I will have to miss next Saturday's lesson, as Emma and I will be away in Chicago, hoping to make a plan for our musical, *The Medium at Large*.

"Good luck to you, then," Chaim exclaims, his goodwill palpable.

The night is cool. Fall has come early. Our cab noses to the curb, where a crowd is milling. We are on our way to see a performance of a new musical, *Under Fire*. Our friend John Herrera has one of the leads, playing a despotic Central American dictator. The crowd for the show is large and excited. The word is out that the cast is excellent and the direction is very good. There is a buzz of excitement. When the doors to the house are closed an extra twenty minutes, the crowd waits expectantly. When we finally file into the theater, not a seat is left untaken.

I have come to see John's work, but the rest of the cast is well worth watching. Perfectly cast and well directed, the show unfolds with passionate intensity. Set in Central America in the mid-seventies, the book traces the ethics of a star-crossed trio of journalists. A revolution is brewing, set to overthrow a tyrannical regime headed by a charismatic despot played by John. From the first moment he steps onstage, he owns the spotlight. His work is powerful and taut. The audience loves him. Although he has never won a Tony, he has been nominated, and it's easy to see why.

At intermission, the crowd has a happy tone. The show is very good so far, and time has spun past quickly.

The second act of the show is even better than the first. The cast takes its bows to a standing ovation. John spots Emma and me during the applause. He gives us a nod. We will check in with him by phone and see him later in the week.

The doorbell shrills. It is my actor friend, come to drop off the final scene of his play. I open the door and he steps inside. The dogs greet him ecstatically.

"Hello, girls," he greets them back. Charlotte brings him her ratty to throw. Aptly named, her ratty is the rattiest rat dog toy in existence. He tosses it toward a corner, but Charlotte catches it in midair. I tease Emma that her dog has lowbrow taste, like the Hebrew National hot dogs available at the vendors in Central Park. Of all Charlotte's myriad toys, her favorite is, of course, the ratty. She can play endless games of "get the ratty," scurrying across our hardwood floors to catch the rodent mid-flight. Tiger Lily casts a desultory eye on the proceedings. *Who wants a ratty, anyhow?* she asks.

"We can read through the scene out loud," my friend offers. He hands me a sheaf of papers. Emma comes in and perches on a love seat to listen. His enthusiasm is contagious. I serve as his catcher's mitt, reading whatever comes over the plate. His first drafts are not polished but still passionate. I enjoy reading him.

So now we launch into the final scene. It's a little intimidating to read with him. He is a formidable actor. His cold reading is, in fact, red-hot. I try not to compare myself, just to read what's on the page. And what is on the page is very good. If he hadn't been called to be an actor, my friend could easily have been a writer. Late to the game, he finds he loves writing. He has set aside writing time every morning. He can't wait to get to the page.

I like to think I own a certain amount of skill, but I don't really feel my native talents outstrip his. I have been writing longer but not necessarily better. Thanks to his work with *The Artist's Way*, he's just starting to write in his mid-fifties. He brings a beginner's excitement and purity to the act. I am for him a mentor and a Muse. I am proud to serve either function. His writing is that good.

It is a windy fall day. We are scheduled to fly out to Chicago. Once there, we will attend a surprise birthday party for Turtle Wax heiress and theatrical powerhouse Sondra Healy and meet with David Bell, our director of choice for *The Medium at Large*. I am a nervous flyer, and my nerves are made worse by the wind. We take off smoothly but then hit bumps as we climb to our cruising altitude of thirty-five thousand feet. If I let myself feel it, I am terrified. I don't want to feel my feelings, so I turn to the stack of tabloids I have brought for distraction. Soon I am absorbed in the latest Hollywood gossip. There is the relationship of Brad Pitt and Angelina Jolie, easily more turbulent than my air flight. Pitt has moved to a separate wing of their French estate, the tabloids report. Also, he is drinking too much, they add.

I find myself reading with empathy and compassion. I, too, overdrank in Hollywood. I was lucky enough to get sober. I wish Pitt the same good fortune if indeed he does have a problem, but the odds are stacked against him. His fame and perceived power will likely prevent him from facing his addiction. He is surrounded by enablers. More's the pity.

A few more jarring bumps and we descend for landing. I mutter a prayer of gratitude as we taxi to the gate. It is as cold and windy in Chicago as it was in New York. I wrap my coat close around me as I tug my suitcase to the curb where Sharee Pemberton, our producer, is waiting. Emma and I heft our suitcases into the back of Sharee's Lexus. We climb into the car, where we are met by a longtime friend of Sharee's. I am numb with travel fatigue and unable to respond much to this woman's monologue.

At the Whitehall Hotel, a small, posh, old-fashioned hotel, Emma and I are given a room with one king-sized bed.

It is Marathon weekend in Chicago, and we are lucky to get a room at all. In all our years of working and traveling together, Emma and I have never shared a bed. As we check in, Sharee is horrified and apologetic, changing us to a double room for the next night. We laugh it off, but I am relieved when I see how huge the bed is. There's more than enough room for both us.

After "dibbing" one side of the bed, I dial the phone number I know by heart for my old, good girlfriend Judge Michele Lowrance. As luck would have it, she is home and able to meet me for dinner.

"The Whitehall has a good restaurant; I'll meet you in twenty minutes," Michele proposes. With that settled, I dial another number I know by heart, another old and good girlfriend, Laura Leddy. We arrange to meet at twelve thirty the next day, again at the hotel's restaurant. There's just enough time to fuss over my makeup and go downstairs to meet Michele.

At the restaurant, I am the first to arrive. I am given a corner table, where I order a Pellegrino with lime. Michele arrives, breathless and beautiful. She orders a Pellegrino, then reaches into her bag and emerges with a book. I take the book in hand, eagerly. It is a bound galley for Michele's first book, *The Good Karma Divorce*.

"Congratulations!" I exclaim. I had a hand in getting the book published. I introduced Michele to my literary agent, Susan Raihofer. Susan loved the book and helped Michele to shape it. Then she sold it for top dollar to a perfect press for it, HarperOne.

We both order salmon, feeling virtuous to turn aside the restaurant's signature pizza. I have known Michele for twenty-five years, and our conversation has ease built into it. Michele was a bridesmaid when I married Mark Bryan. In our wedding pictures, she is a radiant young beauty. Two decades later, she is a beauty still.

"Three years of life as a hermit," Michele declares. "The writer's life is hard, although you must be used to it."

"It's all I've ever known," I tell Michele.

The next morning, I wake to a full day of social visits. My Morning Pages are grumpy because I feel rushed—I have slept in and now have to hurry to pack and move to a different room before my first appointment with Laura Leddy. Laura is a tall, statuesque blonde. She arrives at the Whitehall clad in black jeans and a black sweater. Her blond hair falls in gentle waves just to her shoulders.

"Hello," she carols when she spots me.

"Hello to you," I echo back. We make our way to the restaurant with its low amber lights. Seated again at a table for two, I take in Laura's glamour.

"It's so good to see you," she says.

"And good to see you," I reply.

Laura laments some added weight, but to my eye she looks merely voluptuous, not heavy. A retired teacher of gifted students, she keeps her hand in with some private tutoring. She tells me about a recent intake interview she did with a boy who was only three and just wanted to play. His parents were ambitious on his behalf. Laura found them *too* ambitious.

"I mean, he's only three!" she exclaimed. "He *should* just want to play!"

I tell Laura about the class I am teaching in New York—a batch of skeptics. They are pridefully intellec-tual, which makes them difficult to teach. It takes all of my teaching experience just to counter their "show me, prove it to me" attitude. And I want so to like them.

"Why did they take the course if they're not open to your ideas?" Laura wonders.

"I can't answer that," I reply. "I think it might just take longer for them to break through. I hope so. Their very smartness becomes a block. Just last week, a student raised her hand and announced to the whole class that she was getting absolutely nothing out of the course."

"*What?*" Laura laughs with shock. "What did you say?"

"I told her that if she were doing Morning Pages and Artist Dates, she had to be experiencing a shift, even if she didn't recognize it."

"That's true. I'll pray for both of you."

When I lived in Chicago twenty years ago, Laura was

my prayer partner. We practiced a technique known as Master Minding, in which we visualized each other's prayer requests as successfully realized. Master Minding was very powerful and very intimate. Laura knew my secret heart, and as I talk to her now, I find myself secret-sharing again. I find myself confessing that my class is daunting. Teacher that she is, Laura knows how I feel. I know she will pray for me about my teaching.

"Julie B., Julie B., Julia Bernice," carols my brother Christopher, as he steps into the hotel room. Laura has gone, leaving nothing but good feelings in her wake. Christopher now towers in the doorway. He is my "little" brother, but he's nearly a full foot taller than I am.

"Come in, come in," I urge him.

"It's Julia Bernice," he sings in his pleasant baritone.

He steps closer and envelops me in a brotherly hug. We settle down to talk. He has just produced a CD of his songs: *Jambon*. He has sunk his savings into the project, and so far the feedback is positive. People love the CD and want to know when and where they can see the Jambon band live. There's a gig planned for Boulder, Colorado, the epicenter of the CD's fan base.

"For years I dodged the bullet, but now I have to be the leader," Christopher explains. Despite its costs, he has no regrets about the CD, feeling that the music speaks for itself. A Grammy-nominated keyboard player whose credits include John Mayall, David Letterman, Mavis Staples, and scores of other distinguished collaborators—chief among them, for a long stint, Sonia Dada—Christopher has now tossed his hat into the ring as a band leader, songwriter, and producer. It's a roll of the dice. He tells me of a recent gig where his lead singer arrived with two minutes to spare. As band leader, he has the job of rounding up all his talented players and getting them to the gig on time. "Two minutes," Christopher emphasizes. His stomach lurches at the memory.

"I love your album," I say.

"CD," Christopher corrects me.

"Your CD, I love it."

"Well, that's your job. You're my sister." But my praise clearly pleases him.

We talk for the better part of an hour, with each of us egging the other on to further creative adventures. Both of us are proud of our risk-taking, and proud of each other.

The next evening is the birthday party, and we dress to the nines to celebrate. Chicago's Rush Street is a short strip crammed with nightlife. Gibsons is a first-rate steak joint where movers and shakers congregate. We are in a party room on Gibsons' second floor. It is a surprise party for Sondra Healy. A hundred and one people are jammed into the upper room. When Sondra enters on the arm of her husband, Denis Healy, she is mobbed by grandchildren and a crowd of adult well-wishers.

"Happy birthday! Surprise! Happy birthday!" carols the crowd. Sondra is clearly shocked and overwhelmed. She dabs at her mascara.

"Happy birthday, Grandma," a little one shrills. Sondra throws wide her arms for a hug. There are a dozen grandchildren, and they climb her like a tree. She is a tiny woman, and she is soon engulfed. Waiters begin to circulate with platters of hors d'oeuvres. There is an open bar, and a flute of champagne at every place setting. The dinner menu offers chicken, salmon, filet mignon, and New York strip steaks, Gibsons' specialty. After milling through the good-natured hubbub, Sondra takes her seat and the crowd follows suit. Dinner is served and conversation dips as the crowd focuses on their entrées. My steak is delicious, as is my cheese-topped baked potato. For forty-five minutes, the diners tuck in, and the steak house more than lives up to its reputation. After dinner, it's time to celebrate.

Actor Roger Anderson steps into the center of the

room. His pianist ripples the keys on an upright piano. Roger sings out, "Let her eat cake . . ." a song from Emma's show *Bunny's Bakery*, with lyrics tailored to Sondra. Two verses in, the crowd begins to clap along. The lyrics are infectious.

> *Let her eat cake, let her have more,*
> *All she can take, frosting galore . . .*
> *Make no mistake: cake is what birthdays are for!*
> *Let her eat cake, cake we adore,*
> *Sondra, it's you we're singing for.*
> *So let her eat cake, let her eat cake, and let her have more.*

As Roger wraps up the song with a special thank-you to Emma, Sondra blows out the cake's single candle. A waiter whisks the cake away to a side table, where it is sliced to serve the crowd. Everyone gets a slice of chocolate cake with chocolate-mousse frosting and a garnish of apple pie. In addition to her slice of cake, Sondra has a table laden with presents; with friends rallied round, logging another birthday isn't so bad after all.

Along with Sharee, we are invited to breakfast at Marlys Beider's home. Marlys is a new friend we've met through Sharee and Sondra, and "home" is a posh apartment on Chicago's Gold Coast. The windows are shirred in chiffon and silk. Tall glassed-in cabinets house Dresden figurines. Marlys greets us riding one-legged on a scooter. She is in recovery from surgery, and the scooter looks festive. Marlys herself looks festive, a tall, willowy, platinum blonde. She scoots ahead of us into her oversized kitchen. We take our places on an overstuffed couch. The pillows are so deep, they invite a catnap.

"I took your word for it, Sharee, and made something light," Marlys says. She serves delicate bowls piled high with fruit salad and yogurt.

"Delicious," I tell her, and she beams. Hospitality is important to her. She is glad to serve us seconds after we devour the first bowl.

"So tell me about your play," Marlys urges us. We tell her the story of *The Medium at Large*. We hit the high points: ghosts, 1938, New York.

"I love it," Marlys says encouragingly. "I could sink my teeth and my money into that."

Emma and I are thrilled by this response. Marlys scoots off and comes back with two copies of her novel, *Continuum*. She gives one to me and one to Emma.

"It's good," Sharee tells us. For several years, she and Marlys were partners in a writers' circle. Sharee wrote a thriller, *Murder in Winnetka*, while Marlys wrote *Continuum*. Having done the hard work of writing their own books, both women are generous to us. We talk happily for nearly three hours, until Marlys says, "It's lunchtime. What about some bagels, cream cheese, and salmon?"

"We don't want you to go to any trouble," says Sharee.

"Oh, it's no trouble," declares Marlys. And so we settle in to eat a second time.

"Delicious," I say again, savoring the salmon.

"Really, really good," Emma chimes in.

"You're sure you won't have more?" asks Marlys. I accept her offer. The salmon is really spectacular.

"We'll get you a script and a demo," Sharee volunteers.

"Wonderful," says Marlys. We finish our lunch and take our leave, clutching books in hand.

Heading back to Sondra's house, we are excited to meet with a prospective director, David H. Bell. He is our director of choice for *The Medium at Large*. He has a special knack for period comedy. He directs with a snap, crackle, and pop energy that is precisely what our play calls for. When he meets with us, he brims with optimism, opening the meeting by assuring us of his desire to work with us.

"We want to work with you, too," we respond.

The meat of the meeting comes next, when David asks us to come up with a new opening number, one that propels the action forward into the heart of the play. We hear his ideas with great openness. There's no point in resisting. His ideas sound "right." I glance at Emma and see that she is excited. I feel that way, too.

David has three shows opening by the end of the year. We tell him we will have a rewrite to him within a month. That timing sounds good to him. We end our meeting on an upbeat note. There is work to do, and we all love that prospect.

Sharee, Sondra, Marlys, Tyler, and David are the beginning of a wonderful team—Chicago is known as a great theater town, and we are seeing why. It is hard leaving Chicago. I wish we could whisk them all back to New York. Emma and Tyler hate saying good-bye to each other, and who could blame them? When they are together, they accomplish great swaths of work. Music pours forth.

For my part, I hate leaving my good girlfriends in addition to leaving Tyler, David Bell, and our producer, Sharee Pemberton. Sharee and I have known each other for twenty years, and she assures me that we will be able to work long-distance. "That's what phones are for," she kids me.

Tonight we have a conference call with Sharee. We start the call at seven thirty and it lasts until ten p.m. We get all the way through the show, tweaking here and there, double-checking that we are true to the period, 1938. Emma is meticulous about verisimilitude. She catches many anach-ronisms. She and Sharee work like a pair of pincers. I am outflanked.

I remember the axiom my mother taught: "In order to be a good writer, you must be willing to murder your dar-lings." My "darlings" are sent to the guillotine as Emma and Sharee run a fine-tooth comb through the script. Emma kids me that I have a lurid, sexual imagination. She says we're going along fine writing for Cary Grant until—splat!—I try to slip in a line for Will Ferrell. My jokes are funny, but they're not "period." I trust both Emma and Sharee, and when they are in agreement, I do listen.

On one point we all agree: we need a new opening number. We must find a scene that launches us quickly into the play. It must have action and drama. What can it be? We all like the idea of starting with a car wreck. Boom! The

parents are dead. We go to their funeral and find them squab-
bling, quite alive in the afterlife. The sisters, another pair of
squabblers, are next to take the stage. They squabble all the
way to the medium's house. Presto. An opening. Would this
work? I think we can try it out. There are several songs I
don't want to lose. Perhaps I can write a new song that is
kind of an umbrella, a container for the other songs. We will
see. I may need to murder some more darlings.

I have a dinner date with Peter at our usual café. I am eager
to hear his new adventures. I have an hour to go before I
leave, and it is filled with music. All day long Emma has been
at work on her new show, *The Blue Lobster*. It is a show
about friendship. Emma first heard music and then lyrics.
Now she is at work marrying the two together. So far the
songs sound marvelous. In fact, they sound so good that

Charlotte is distracted from the incoming storm. I myself am reluctant to leave.

Just as I exit the apartment building, the deluge comes as promised. Water teems in the streets. My umbrella is scant protection. I scurry into the vegetarian café. The waiter waves hello and signals me to Peter's and my regular table. I slip out of my wet coat and prop my umbrella at an angle against the wall. Peter arrives, breathless and drenched. He peels off his jacket and his sweater. His black T-shirt is still dry.

"Hello," he says, bending down to give me a kiss.

"Hello," I echo.

"So tell me about Chicago," he asks.

I tell him Chicago was intense. Bringing on new collaborators speeds up the process and is at once exciting and grueling. My work on the musical is not over yet. There is a need for a whole new opening number.

"It sounds hard," Peter says. "But it sounds good. And it may all go with the territory. I think you'll get the show on."

"Thank you. Your voice to God's ear," I respond.

Peter has taken a job doing sound design for a down-town theater. He enjoys the show, an illusionist's one-man show. He also has continued to study acting with veteran teacher Jerry Brody. As he talks about Brody's class, his face lights up. It is then that I notice his striking resem-blance to Jean-Paul Belmondo.

"I've been writing a little, too," Peter tells me. "I've got three scenes done. I'm hoping Jerry will pick one of them for the next class."

At age fifty-five, Peter has an exciting life due to his willingness to be a beginner. For twenty-five years, he worked as a sound engineer, designing recording studios. When the advances in computer programs dried up that revenue source, he turned to teaching audio. When the recession bit into that resource, he turned to theater work, coming belatedly to a love of acting and writing. I admire Peter for his courage and resilience.

"How's your writing going?" Peter wants to know.

"It comes in dribs and drabs," I answer. Then I decide

that sounds too negative. "It is coming," I say. "Just more slowly than I would like."

"It's a process?" Peter gently kids, but he nods sympathetically. We signal the waiter and order two Zen platters.

Over our salads, we talk about the need for faith.

"I feel like we need to have faith—or at least act as if we have faith," Peter ventures.

"I think it's true that faith requires a leap into the unknown," I respond.

"And some leaps are bigger than others." Peter grins.

I laugh at his candor. "I think, cornered by circumstances, we do leap, and we're both cornered by circumstances right now. But I think we're both safe."

Now it's Peter's turn to laugh. I tell him, "I'm sixty-one years old, a veteran writer, I still get scared, and I am safe. But 'leap and the net will appear' has held up so far . . ."

Peter meets my eyes. "I'll bring you a scene to look at," he promises. For Peter, sharing his fledgling work feels like a risk. I am pleased when he feels safe enough to take it.

Ordinarily, seeing Domenica once a week is "enough," but not this week. It is Sunday, and I find myself yearning for a good mother-daughter visit. I call Domenica to see if she can meet me for dinner.

"That sounds delightful," she responds when I broach my plan.

"Seven thirty at Bella Luna?" I ask.

"You've got it," she answers with a snap.

And so at seven thirty I step into Bella Luna, a casual, friendly, and delicious neighborhood restaurant. "Boo!" says Domenica, who beat me to the spot. I ask for a table for two for dinner, and we are led to a choice table.

"So hello," I say once we're seated.

"Hello," Domenica responds.

"Let's order, then talk," I propose. We both know what we want. I want mezzo, a cold plate of assorted appetizers, and then skirt steak on a bed of tomatoes and arugula. Domenica will share my mezzo and then have salmon carpaccio for her entrée. As we place our orders, our waiter nods his approval.

"So how are you?" I ask Domenica.

"You're being awfully quiet," she responds, a little bit suspiciously.

"I realized I was missing you. Seeing you last Wednesday was great, but it wasn't enough," I tell her. At our last gathering, Domenica brought her computer and showed me some footage she had shot in Maine. The footage looked wonderful: striking and haunting. Domenica plans to have the film cut together before Christmas. She is excited by the work and cautiously optimistic. Now I want to hear more.

Satisfied that my silence springs from curiosity, Domenica debriefs me about her shoot. It went so well that she fantasizes about her collaborators becoming a "pod" who work together project to project, mutually supportive. I do not think this fantasy is so far-fetched.

"It went really, really well. When we were losing light, I told everybody that we didn't have much time left, and they really buckled down. We actually ended up wrapping early." Domenica's voice is calm and well satisfied. Clearly, she loves directing.

"How's your editor?" I ask.

"I hope she's fine. We start cutting midway through next week when she's wrapped everything else on her plate. I'm hoping to make a paper cut quickly to act as a map."

Our mezzo arrives, and then our entrées. Before I know it, Domenica and I are sipping after-dinner cappuccinos.

"Dessert?" I ask her. "Tartufo?"

"I had half a cannoli earlier," she says, sipping at the foam on her cappuccino. "And I've got a shoot coming up, so I have to watch it."

Domenica is an actor-director-writer, and actor is up next.

My doorbell shrills, and the dogs launch into a bedlam of greeting. My colleague and friend, James Nave, steps into the room, ushering his girlfriend, Tish Valles, into the living room. Nave and I taught together for several years. This is the first time I am meeting Tish, although they have been together nearly five years. They make a striking couple. Nave has a shaved head and dark, lively eyes. Tish is half Filipino and half Spanish, a sloe-eyed beauty.

"Come in, come in," I invite them. The dogs swirl at their feet.

"So, Julia, you look good," Nave announces.

"A little older, a little heavier," I tell him. We all take seats on one leather sofa and matching love seat. I am curious about Tish. She is a high-powered advertising consultant. In her years with Nave, she has been stationed in Bangkok, Manila, and now New York. I had expected her to be hard-edged, but instead she is calm, self-effacing, and feminine. Clearly still smitten with Nave. And with Nave, there is a lot to like. He is a cofounder of Poetry Alive, an outreach program that sends teams of poets into schools to perform live poetry. He has a master's degree in poetry and keeps his hand in as a performance poet. He teaches both creative writing and creativity workshops. His friendships span the globe.

"How is your French?" Nave asks me now. "I've been teaching creativity workshops in Paris, half in English, half in French."

"My French is pretty rudimentary," I tell Nave.

"Are you hungry?" he asks.

"*Oui, j'ai faim,*" I reply, reasonably sure he will get the idea.

We settle on Jackson Hole, the "home of the seven-ounce burger." It's a scant block from my apartment, and it features a delicious cucumber-yogurt soup.

"I'm writing," Nave tells me as we settle in. "I think it's a book. It's just taking shape of its own accord."

"It's great you're writing a book," I tell him. I have enjoyed Nave's writing in many genres. His prose is as strong as his poetry. Nave's plan is winter in New York, then back out to Taos for late spring and summer.

"Taos has become a writer's mecca," he tells me. He describes the new café and coffee bar that is ideal for writing. "You'd love it," he concludes, knowing that I made a habit of writing in Dori's Bakery, now defunct.

"Do you still have that storage unit?" Nave asks.

"I do."

"There were all kinds of things in it," he recalls. "Lots of copies of your poetry album, some good paintings, I can't remember what else."

"I should ship it all to New Jersey," I say, saddened by the conversation. Leaving Taos was one of the hardest things I've ever done. My heart loved the beauty there, but it was not a safe place for me. I've been gone nearly ten years now, and there is still an ache when I think of the sage fields and the beautiful flank of Taos mountain dappled by the sun.

"Maybe if you went just for a brief vacation," Nave ventures. "If you could just go to see your friends and the scenery."

"Emma thinks Taos is dangerous for me," I tell him.

Indeed, Emma visibly shudders whenever I mention

missing Taos. I had a very severe breakdown there, and Emma soldiered through it alone without adequate medical help. She has never forgotten how bad and how frightening it was.

"I don't think I'll be going back anytime soon," I tell Nave. "I don't really think it's safe."

"If you weren't working?" he asks. He thinks the stress of work brought on my breakdown.

"I just don't think it's a good idea. You'll have to enjoy Taos for me."

"I can do that," Nave relents. Our conversation veers into less volatile territory. I tell him my current creativity class is difficult to teach—the students are too smart for their own good. He remembers several different classes that he found hard—one in New Haven, two in Santa Fe.

"I keep thinking Santa Fe might be an alternative to Taos," I confess sheepishly.

"No, no, you wouldn't like it. It's a lot of trust-fund babies who are wannabe artists," Nave declares, still stung by the memory.

"It doesn't sound very appetizing," I allow.

"Trust me. It's not," Nave says decisively. He looks out the window at the New York passersby. "You're better off here," he concludes. Our hamburgers arrive.

At a quarter to two, my doorbell sounds. It is Chaim, fifteen minutes early.

"Hello, Julia," he greets me. "I hope it is OK that I'm early. I brought some coffee but no cream."

"I've got some, and it's good to see you," I tell him. We perch at the table near the living-room window. I pour coffee for both of us, adding French vanilla creamer to my cup.

"This is delicious coffee," I tell Chaim.

"I got it at a coffee bar on the East Side," he tells me. "Then I carried it with me on the bus. It was nerve-racking on the bus. All of the children were keyed up by Halloween. The racket!"

"I love Halloween," I tell him.

"Not I. It's a whole holiday devoted to witchcraft." Chaim grimaces and makes claws of his hands. "No, I don't like it."

"Halloween is fun," I protest. I remind Chaim of the costumes down in the Village. Sixth Avenue is bedlam.

"This is Halloween," Chaim says, crossing the room to the piano, where he picks out some spooky music. I have to laugh. The music does sound like Halloween.

"Shall we begin?" Chaim asks. He turns to a piece he himself composed, "The Winter's Tale." I pick it out, a little unevenly. We play it through several times before moving on to "The Old Church," another original.

"What's this?" Chaim asks, picking up a sheet of music.

"It's *Romeo and Juliet*," I exclaim. "I love that music."

"Yes, it has a swagger to it. The two families are dancing, but you can feel their adversity in the music." Chaim gets to his feet and demonstrates. I laugh at his antics.

"Let's give it a try," he says, and I go at the music. We play it through several times with minor stumbles.

"You play it once," I beg him. With great zest, Chaim plays the piece through. It is delicious.

"Let me play you a piece of music from an old Russian movie called *The Storm.*" With great glee, Chaim plays a tumultuous piece of music. It has some of the same swagger as Prokofiev's *Romeo and Juliet.*

"I love that," I say. "Maybe I really like Russian music."

"Have you ever been to Russia?"

"No, never."

"I have. Saint Petersburg is a wonderful city. The architecture is not to be believed, and they have these canals."

"I didn't know about the canals."

"Oh, yes."

"Shall we try?" Chaim cues up the music to another piece of his called "Autumn Song." We play it through just once. I know it well.

"Have you seen the ballet?" Chaim wonders. He is back to *Romeo and Juliet*.

"No, I haven't," I tell him.

"Well, then, we will have to go next spring."

"I'd love to."

"Now, enough for today?" Chaim asks.

"Enough. But I love the *Romeo and Juliet*."

"Yes. It is wonderful music."

Chaim puts the sheet music back into its purple folder. He tucks the folder into a sideboard.

"One day, I'll make you a dinner. A feast," he promises.

"I'd love that," I say as I usher him to the door.

***

Manhattan is studded with theater spaces available for rental. John Herrera has chosen a space on Fifty-second

Street, between Ninth and Tenth avenues. The occasion is a first read-through of his *Las Abuelas*. The crowd is a combination of well-wishers and critics. I feel that I am a little bit of both.

The reading kicks off at three fifteen. John has gathered a worthy group of actors, and they bite into the play with gusto. The play is an ensemble piece about an extended Cuban family. The difficult and domineering matriarch is drawn clearly. So are a pair of star-crossed lovers and the gay uncle who helps them to elope. John pulls no punches in his writing. Episode upon episode unfolds laden with drama. The play's first act is too long, an hour and forty-five minutes. We take a ten-minute break, then start again. The second act unfurls more rapidly, coming in at about an hour. The play spans twenty-five years. We watch two generations take center stage. Their lives are fraught with tension.

The reading ends just at six. There is no time for audience feedback. The room is rented to another playwright. Another new play will try to find its legs. John thanks everyone for coming. With the reading over, he is the hospitable host, no longer the nervous author. I kiss him good-bye, pleased to have been a part of his creative process.

I am slated to teach two workshops in London. They are under the auspices of Alternatives, London's leading venue for holistic learning. Emma likes the feel of the Alternatives crew by phone and e-mail. With any luck, all should go smoothly. We are to be billeted at a small, posh hotel, the Dorset Square Hotel. I have stayed there once before and remember loving its comfortable and striking rooms. When Emma and I arrive, we are not disappointed. Our room has crimson walls, almost an exact match for the color of my walls in my bedroom at home.

"This is great," I say to Emma. "I'm going to be very comfortable here." We have a few hours' rest before we go to meet our hosts for tea. I opt for a nap; Emma opts for a walk around the neighborhood. When I wake at two, Emma is back and elated. The neighborhood has proved itself interesting. She has spotted Madame Tussauds and Starbucks. She has stopped in a greengrocer and bought water and Ribena, a black-currant concentrate. She is ready to head off to tea.

Tea convenes at a posh teahouse. We have tiny little sandwiches and scones with clotted cream and strawberry preserves. Conversation eddies amiably up and down the table. We learn that Esther, the programmer who invited us to teach, is a playwright herself. Tom, another key staff member, reveals himself as a painter. He hands around postcards of his work. It is marvelous. We stay at tea until six, eager to make a real connection. When we disperse, it has started raining. We spend a half-hour flagging a taxi, a minute's transaction back home.

I opt to eat dinner in our room; Emma dashes straight back out into the storm. She is bound to see *War Horse*, a production recommended by our friend Judy Collins. I head for early bed, wanting to be well rested to teach.

The next morning, I stir just as Emma returns from a run to Starbucks. She has brought me two large iced coffees and a blueberry yogurt. I down them all, rush through my Morning Pages, dress, and am ready to teach. I face a crowd of three hundred fifty people, all eager to work with *The Artist's Way* tools. Fully half of them are working with the tools already.

"I'm going to teach Morning Pages," I tell the crowd. "If you're doing them already, please just feel smug."

This said, I launch into teaching. The crowd is a lively one, filled with questions. For the better part of an hour, I answer their queries, then I move on to exercises. I ask many questions, then break the crowd into clusters of three so they can compare their answers and "steal" from one another. The clusters bubble with energy. I teach for six hours using the clustering technique. By day's end, the crowd is well satisfied and so am I. It is rewarding to teach a group as open and receptive as this one. One day down and one to go, I am no longer apprehensive. I look forward to day two.

The second teaching day looms ahead of me. The hall rented for day two is dark and narrow. I cannot see the audience although they can see me. It's a strain for me to teach into the void. I try to focus on doing my job well. By midday, the crowd is humming along happily. I teach different tools from yesterday, although their goal is the same: to unlock creativity. By day's end, the group is buzzing. They happily cluster and debrief their findings. The tools work well.

After the long day's teaching, it's my turn to debrief with Esther and Tom, the Alternatives team. I tell them I am greatly pleased, that I feel both days went well but that I strongly preferred the venue for day one, which was brightly lit and spacious.

"So we know for next year," Tom says.

"We'd love to have you back," Esther says.

"I'd love to come back," I tell them.

It's five o'clock on Sunday when I finish teaching. London's theaters are dark on Sunday, so we need to devise a different adventure. "Why not go to Chinatown?" Tom asks us. He explains that London's Chinatown resembles San Francisco's. He suggests a restaurant, Golden Dragon, where many Chinese people dine. It's on Gerrard Street, Chinatown's main drag.

I am tired from teaching, but the idea of an adventure tempts my heart. Emma and I ask our hotel's porter to flag us a cab. We get in and ask for Chinatown. The cab winds its way through tiny back streets, shortcuts to Gerrard Street. We thank our cabbie and disembark. The sidewalks are crowded with people; clearly we are not the only ones who sought adventure by coming to Chinatown. We walk several blocks up Gerrard Street, keeping our eyes peeled for Golden Dragon. We pass the Golden Phoenix, and we keep on trusting that Tom has the name right. Finally, yes, we spot it. We enter and find ourselves in a cavernous space filled with round tables, all occupied.

"Two for dinner," we tell the hostess.

"I take you upstairs," she replies, leading us up a steep stairway to the second floor, also crowded, also cavernous. There is an empty table, and she ushers us to it. Leaving us with menus, she disappears. The menus are voluminous. We leaf through them, looking for familiar entrées. I suggest we get the appetizer sampler. Emma agrees. We each order a separate entrée. Our waitress worries that our choices are "too Chinese." We won't like them, she fears. Emma and I stick to our guns. Our years of Chinese dining in New York have prepared us well.

Our appetizers arrive, and we make short work of them. One table over, a Chinese couple with a baby in tow take their seats. The baby is very beautiful and very placid. There are no tears and no fussing. Emma laughs and says that her friend, a new mother, has recently bought a book on Asian child-rearing techniques for Caucasians—their children are so much better behaved than ours.

Our entrées arrive and, despite our waitress's concerns, they prove delicious to us. I have ordered spicy prawns. They arrive drowned in a red-pepper sauce. They are zesty and very good. Emma has ordered a tofu-based soup. It, too, is delicious.

"This is a good adventure," I tell Emma between mouthfuls.

"Yes," says Emma. "I'm glad we came."

We demur dessert, pay our tab, and retreat to the street, where we spot a Chinese bakery with elaborately frosted cakes. We duck inside—everything is a carnival of color. Emma chooses two desserts for us, a slice of banana cake and a pineapple gelatin. Once again, we are lucky. Her choices prove delicious.

"This is a good adventure," I repeat. We flag a cab.

Our flight home is Monday night. We have all day free, and Emma is resolved that we should go to Harrods, the massive department store.

"Even just looking at its windows is a treat," Esther tells us. So when the cab lets us off opposite an entrance, we don't go in. Instead, we make a circuit of the store's windows, all based on *The Wizard of Oz*. Window by window, the tale is told. We meet the Scarecrow, the Tin Man, Dorothy, and Toto. We spot the ruby slippers. By the time we've traveled the windows' full circuit, our heads are stuffed full of images: the yellow brick road, the Emerald City. We finally enter the store and find ourselves in the watch room, which feels like an acre of timepieces ranging from the reasonable up through the very expensive. The very expensive watches tended to be fanciful. "I Serpenti," one collection was dubbed, and its watches did resemble serpents.

Up the escalator several floors, we come upon The Pet Kingdom. There are a half-dozen glass-enclosed viewing stations featuring rabbits, hamsters, and dachshund puppies. Emma gravitates toward a cache of glittery dog collars. She selects a bright red collar studded with rhinestones. "Charlotte could use a new collar," she explains, picking out a red leash to go with the collar.

Back on the escalator, this time we disembark at the Christmas Room. I love all the ornaments, and I pick out half a dozen for our Christmas tree. Emma, too, selects a spate of the glittery finery. We will have a grand Christmas tree this year. Emma has chosen a red velvet teapot embroidered "Harrod's 2009." It will go to her mother, who was living in England when Emma was born.

"Imagine if I still had my British accent," Emma says. She lived in England until she was five but lost her accent within two weeks of returning to America. "My mother was so disappointed," she recalls.

Harrods is thronged with holiday shoppers although the holiday season has scarcely begun. The crowd jostles and bumps to a litany of apologies. "Excuse me," "Pardon me," "Sorry." We make our way to Gourmet Foods, where jams, jellies, preserves, and chocolates tempt the palate. Emma is a fine baker, and she lustfully surveys the scope of gourmet

—————————— ❦ ——————————

ingredients. I have to tug her by her sleeve: time to go. We catch a cab back to our hotel, where we collect our luggage and catch another cab out to Heathrow. Our trip is ending.

❦

It's one forty-five p.m. and I am on the phone with Gerard Hackett, my friend of forty years. I am still in pajamas and curlers. I fell asleep at about three a.m. The doorbell sounds a short, imperious hoot.

"Gerard, it's my doorbell and I'm not decent. Can I call you back?"

"Sure you can."

"Thanks. Good-bye."

Who could it be? I wonder, then I remember: Chaim, piano lesson! I buzz him up, but I tell him, "I'm still in my pajamas."

"You look wonderful," Chaim says as I open the door

—————————— ❦ ——————————

to him. I am wearing plaid men's pajamas from L.L.Bean. I've wrapped my head with a towel. A glance in the mirror tells me I look a little wild. Chaim, as always, is handsome and well dressed.

"Take your time," he tells me. "I'm in no hurry. I am early."

A glance at the clock tells me this is so. It's ten to two; our lesson starts at two.

"I won't be long, I promise," I say, retreating to my bedroom, where I doff my pajamas and climb into some soft black slacks and a top. Next I race into makeup, and last I brush through my hair. Presentable? Yes, barely. I rejoin Chaim.

"I brought you some hot coffee," he says. "It may take more cream. Shall I get some from the refrigerator?"

"Yes, that would be great."

"So tell me about London," Chaim urges.

"It was wonderful," I answer. "Our flight was wonderful, our hotel was wonderful, my seminars were wonderful."

"I'm so glad. I had a feeling that they would be," Chaim says.

"Emma went to the theater twice, and together we went to Chinatown and Harrods."

"That's in Knightsbridge, right?"

"Right."

"Did you get anything there?"

"Christmas ornaments, and Emma got Charlotte a new collar, bright red and studded with rhinestones."

"Ah, yes, I see it now." Chaim reaches out to give Charlotte an affectionate pat. Charlotte wants to play "throw the ratty," but Chaim has an eye on the clock.

"Not now, Charlotte," he says, and then to me, "Shall we get started? I have a new Russian piece I'd like to play you."

Chaim crosses to the piano. Like him, it is tall, dark, and handsome, a Petrof, a little-known brand that is excellent.

"You didn't make a mistake buying this piano," Chaim comments. "It has the sound of a grand."

I bought the piano at the suggestion of pianist Bob

McDonald's Steinway technician. I wanted a piano good enough and big-enough-sounding for Bob McDonald to play. Chaim, too, was a concert pianist in his youth, and the piano sounds happy under his touch. Settling in at the keys, he plays a melancholic melody.

"I like it," I say, and Chaim jots down the melody. I try it out but realize we have a piece of music I like much better. "Will you play the Prokofiev *Romeo and Juliet?*" I ask Chaim.

"But of course," he replies, and soon his hands are swaggering across the keys. Chaim plays with great brio. I absolutely love the bravura technique he brings to the piece. Now it is my turn at the keys. I pick out the notes tentatively but with growing enthusiasm.

"I just *love* this piece," I say.

"Yes, I can hear that," Chaim says. "Shall we play it again?"

It's a red-letter day today. I received my copies of *Photoplay*, a chapbook of poems by my friend Julianna McCarthy. The little book is handsome. The poems are tough-minded yet romantic. There is a blurb from me on the back cover. I quote it now:

> As memorable as a great film noir, McCarthy's poems have an insider's grit. She catches it all from the paparazzo's grabbed shot to the study by Hurrell. *Photoplay* lives up to its name.

In order to write the blurb, I read the book in manuscript form. It was very good then, but through the alchemy of being a published book, it is now that much better. The transformation is familiar to me after publishing thirty-plus books myself, but the change still feels magical. Then, too, there is the fact that Julianna herself is magical. A lifelong actress, she began writing poetry as she entered her seventies. The process enthralled her and gave her an outlet for her prodigious creative energies. At seventy-five, she enrolled in graduate school. Within two years she received her MFA in poetry. Now eighty, she is widely published. *Photoplay* is her first collection.

The voice of the poems is tough and worldly. The picture of Julianna on the book's cover shows a silver-haired, blue-eyed woman, clearly once a beauty and clearly a beauty still. In the portrait, she stares into the middle distance, as if making a clear-eyed assessment. Perhaps she sees her next book taking form. I've known Julianna for thirty-one years. In that time, her thinking has always surprised and challenged me. It is my hope that it will do the same for her readers.

The crowd in Merkin Hall is largely silver-headed. They've come to enjoy an evening of song. The bill of fare promises to be appetizing: great songwriting teams of the American musical theater. At the suggestion of Emma's friend, composer Lillian Redl, we bought last-minute tickets, and the three of us are perched high in the balcony. The stage below features a Steinway grand piano set upon a Persian rug. The lights dim, and a door to the wings opens. A motorized cart whisks disabled pianist Steven Blier to center stage. He scrambles to the piano stool, flashing a triumphant grin at accomplishing the task. Urbane and witty, he welcomes the audience warmly, then strikes an opening chord as singer Jason Graae steps from the wings. Graae is an ingratiating performer, and his rendition of "Lucky Day" is charming. He has a puckish glee and an antic grace. When he yields the stage to Mary Testa, he is chivalry personified.

Mary Testa is a Tony-nominated Broadway veteran. She is droll and delicious, charming the audience with Rodgers and Hart's "Wait Till You See Him." Testa is so full of moxie the audience could stay with her all night, but instead she yields right of way to Sylvia McNair, a glamorous two-time Grammy winner. McNair is all polish and sass. She completes the trio of singers. The evening spins on with songs from George and Ira Gershwin, Howard Dietz and Arthur Schwartz, Richard Rodgers and Oscar Hammerstein, Harold Arlen and Johnny Mercer, and more. Blier's deft piano arrangements complement the tunes but never overwhelm the singers. His program notes are equally tasty. His wit invites the audience to laugh along.

Emma is spellbound, listening to the great songs unfurling. The teams whose works are sung include Alan Jay Lerner and Frederick Loewe, Jerry Bock and Sheldon Harnick, Richard Maltby and David Shire, William Bolcom and Arnold Weinstein, and Jerry Leiber and Mike Stoller. When the evening ends to thundering applause, the encore is a work by John Kander and Fred Ebb.

"This is what I'm meant to be doing," Emma whispers excitedly as we file out. "I think I should write ninety songs in ninety days again."

"Maybe I'll join you at that," I respond.

Lillian looks pleased. "I'm glad you found this inspiring— I thought you might."

It's a little like entering Santa's workshop. I turn my key in the lock and open the door on Bunny's Bakery—but not the musical—the bakery. Emma's show was born from the true story of her own baking. It is almost Thanksgiving, and this year, she has asked Domenica to be her assistant for the holiday rush. Both wearing aprons and toques, they have set up an assembly line on the dining-room table and are busily assembling pink boxes and lining them with tissue papers. The boxes are delightfully festive. They will each hold a dozen and a half gingersnaps. The heavenly smell wafting from the kitchen is the scent of gingersnap dough.

"Shall we bake a batch just for us?" Emma asks.

"Yes!" Domenica and I chorus in unison.

"Let me show you." Emma ushers Domenica into the kitchen. "This may be a bit tricky. It's much easier once the dough is chilled, but we'll give it a try."

Emma takes a dollop of dough, shapes it into a ball, rolls

the ball in sugar, and places it on a cookie sheet. "Now you try," she urges Domenica.

"The dough is sticking to my fingers!" Domenica exclaims.

"It's much easier chilled," Emma assures her. "But just do the best you can."

"I'll try," Domenica says doubtfully. Her ball of dough isn't really perfectly round, but she rolls it in the sugar and plunks it onto the cookie sheet, pleased to be a help.

"Good. That's the idea," Emma says encouragingly. Together, they work to fill out the cookie sheet.

"How long do these take?" Domenica asks.

"Oh, six to eight minutes," Emma answers, sliding the cookie sheet into the oven. "This batch won't be too pretty," she adds. But seven minutes later when she pulls the cookies out, they look perfect. I am sending gingersnaps for Christmas this year, and I'm well pleased that they are delectable.

Domenica and Emma are talking about Emma's new

musical, *The Blue Lobster*. Emma hops to the piano to play the opening number. Domenica listens intently.

"It has the feel of Elton John, the way the chords open out," she pronounces.

"I love that," Emma says.

They plunge into a discussion of the show. Spatula in hand, Emma sets the cookies to cool one at a time. I eat the first one, still warm. Then I eat two, three, and four. I could eat the full batch, but Emma and Domenica try a cookie apiece and then declare the rest of the batch will go home with Domenica as a treat for her boyfriend. *How could he not be in love with her?* I think to myself.

We are to meet at a restaurant called Harry Cipriani. It is nestled on the ground floor of the Sherry-Netherland hotel on Fifth Avenue between Fifty-ninth and Sixtieth streets. The "we" is my friend Gerard; my daughter, Domenica; Bill and Judy Plott; plus myself. The Plotts are visiting from Boston, and their visit is the cause of our festive luncheon.

I arrive early, and the maître d'hôtel makes a fuss over me, seating me at a table for five. I order a large bottle of sparkling water and settle in to wait. The restaurant bubbles with gaiety. The crowd looks more European than American. Snatches of Italian and French and accented English come from nearby tables. I have a sense of déjà vu, then I realize that the restaurant has supplanted the old Sherry-Netherland bar. I did the last of my drinking there. In fact, my table is situated nearly precisely where my old drinking table was. I sip at my sparkling water, grateful to be sober.

Domenica and Gerard arrive. The Plotts follow close at their heels. Domenica has warned me the menu will be pricey. She has been to Harry's Bar in Venice, Italy. Even forewarned, the menu is a jolt. I choose grilled liver, a specialty of the house, and it costs a cool forty dollars. Gerard's hamburger is twenty-five. Domenica's minestrone, eighteen. Bill and Judy know their way around the menu. They order risotto and veal Milanese.

"We're treating," they announce. Bill orders a sweet vermouth. Gerard asks for a glass of chardonnay. I stick to water, as does Domenica. Judy orders a ginger ale. "To friends," the toast goes up. Gerard, Bill, and I have been friends for forty-plus years. We met as freshmen in college, and I remember Bill from those years as wild. That was before his marriage to Judy and forty years of teaching drama. He is now retired and has turned his hand to writing. I remember he was a fine writer when we were in school. Bill clears his throat and says, "We have something to celebrate." We're all ears as he tells us that his new play has won a staged reading with the Provincetown Players Theater Company. This is good news indeed. It is a prestigious venue, and Bill is a little stunned. "They picked me and some real playwrights," he says.

"Congratulations," I exclaim.

"Congratulations," Gerard and Domenica echo. "To your play!"

"Thank you, thank you," says Bill. He sips at his vermouth, hardly the wild drinker I remember.

"What's its title?" I ask.

"It's called *Ibsen's Bastards*," Bill answers. He explains
that Ibsen had an illegitimate son, and thereafter a strain of
illegitimacy ran in Ibsen's family. Talking about his play,
Bill is modest and self-deprecating. He explains that he has
written three other plays, two one-acts that will be a tril-
ogy, and one other full-length play. From the sound of it, he
loves writing. Now that he's retired from teaching, he has
the time to give to it.

"What are you writing now?" he asks me.

"A nonfiction book," I answer. "A journal."

"Ah," breathes Bill. "Aha."

The talk spins on to other things. Our food arrives,
and with it a lull in the conversation. I steal a glance at Bill,
silver-headed now. Gerard, too, has gray at his temples.
We've all turned out rather well, I think. I sip at my water,
sober and serene.

Twenty-two people crowd our living room. It is Thanksgiving Day, and we have cooked to feed the multitudes. Emma
and Domenica have baked the desserts together, using the
opportunity for Emma to train Domenica in Bunny's techniques. A pumpkin pie, a chocolate-peppermint cake, a ginger cake with chocolate ganache, a chocolate-orange cake,
and three dozen gingersnaps later, Domenica is well schooled.
Additionally, I've baked sour cream–raisin pie from an old
family recipe. I also did an eighteen-pound turkey, sage
dressing, cranberry-cornmeal stuffing, cheesed cream onions,
green-bean-and-mushroom casserole, sweet-potato casserole,
cranberry relish, and biscuits. Emma's mother, Martha, in
for the holiday, made delicious gravy, and her father made
mashed potatoes. Emma's Aunt Jackie brought a cheese
platter and hors d'oeuvres of crab-and-artichoke dip and
stuffed mushrooms, and an orchid plant to grace the table.

Gerard arrives early to carve the turkey using an electric carving knife he inherited from his parents. His sister Virginia arrives moments later bearing a gift, "my usual Godiva." Peter enters carrying ice cream to garnish the desserts. Domenica and her boyfriend arrive, and soon after, Domenica's friends—Johnny bearing flowers, Veronica with her twoandahalfyearold. I retreat to the kitchen to begin ferrying platters out to the table. We are serving smorgasbordstyle, and we use every available inch of the table. Gerard finishes carving and sets out the platters of light meat and dark meat. Peter is first in line, and others crowd close behind him.

Veronica's daughter, Phoenix, makes friends with Charlotte. They retreat to a corner by the piano in a world of their own. Tiger Lily hovers underfoot near the food, hoping for a turkey handout. I spot her and offer her a biscuit. She gobbles it with delight.

Guests perch on the piano bench, overflow the couch and love seat, kneel on the floor. Someone hauls chairs from my bedroom. Conversation eddies from group to group.

I talk with Rob Lively. His theology background gives us much common ground, and we enjoy comparing notes. Laughter rings out from the corner, where Emma is deep in conversation with Tyler's older brother, Todd Beattie. They are egging each other on with outrageous ideas for a new Food Network show. The love seat holds just enough space for my friend John; his partner, Ron; and Steven Fales. Their voices carry all the way across the room as they talk actors' shop.

"Second helpings," Peter announces as he helps himself to another plateful. Once again he's the leader of the pack. Guests crowd the table, angling for second helpings of their favorites. I help myself to more dark meat and sage dressing topped with Martha's gravy. In the kitchen, I fill the gravy boat a second time. Martha's gravy is velvety-smooth and savory. I notice everyone pouring themselves generous dollops.

"Everyone loves the gravy," I tell Martha.

"The turkey was flavorful," she says modestly.

"Attention, attention," John's voice booms out. "It's

time for the desserts, but first let us sing Happy Birthday." Sure enough, Emma has added candles to three of the cakes. She lights them as John counts down and then carols out the "Happy Birthday" song. All the guests sing along with John, but his voice carries the day. Martha, Uncle Bill, and Aunt Jackie lean in and blow out the candles. There is a round of applause, then Emma plucks the candles out and begins to slice the cakes, starting with a slice for each celebrant. Belatedly, I remember Peter's ice cream. I retrieve a half-gallon from the freezer. Each dessert plate now gets a scoop.

Domenica and her boyfriend eat their desserts in a hurry. They are due at the other side of the family, at a restaurant all the way downtown.

"It was great, Mom," Domenica says as she slips into her coat.

No sooner does Domenica leave than actor James Dybas arrives, a friend named Lucky in tow. Both James and Lucky are Broadway veterans. They set about regaling the remaining guests. They met on an industrial show "when we were just kids," James recalls. He sings a lick and leaps to his feet to demonstrate a tap number. "Oh, whoops, your downstairs neighbor!" he exclaims, halting his tap-tap-tapping. Lucky picks up where he leaves off. She is in black, head to toe, including a black-velvet cloche. She teaches dance and yoga, she explains. Aunt Jackie is mesmerized by her résumé. The two of them exchange numbers. Jackie is a portrait artist, and she gravitates to other artists. Lucky basks in her attention.

"We need to hit the road," James announces. He gets to his feet, and Lucky leaps to hers. Grabbing him by the waist, she calls out, "C'mon, kiddo. Shuffle off to Buffalo." They dance their way out the door.

The matinee of *Jersey Boys* has a two p.m. curtain. At one fifteen, I flag a cab on Columbus Avenue. I have allowed an extra half-hour of travel time in case we run into holiday traffic. Surprisingly, the coast is clear and we sail straight down Ninth Avenue to Fifty-second Street and then another long block and a half, also clear, and we're at the theater. I've got my ticket, and I climb three steep flights of stairway one. Winded, I show my ticket to an usher. "Up left and then right," I am advised. I climb another steep set of stairs, turn left into an aisle, then look right to row G. Seat 101 is on the aisle. Emma and her parents are seated farther in.

I take my seat and open the Playbill. I am eager to read the career credits of Bob Crewe, the lyricist. Thirty-two years ago I was a friend to Bob out in Los Angeles. In the years since writing and producing the songs that are featured in *Jersey Boys*, he has become a painter, leaving the music world behind him. I own one of Bob's paintings, and I have coveted several more. Arguably as fine a painter as he was a lyricist, Bob's life is too large to fit into program notes. Just as I close the Playbill, the lights dim.

Jersey Boys is a feel-good show, the story of Frankie Valli and The Four Seasons, and it is a hit parade, crammed with

music. Twenty-two numbers in Act One and nineteen more
in Act Two. The audience knows the songs, mouthing the
words and clapping along. The show is New Jersey proud,
and so is the audience, featuring big hair and a lot of "bling."
Even the eye makeup is different from a New York crowd:
heavier on eyeliner, thicker on mascara. On the men, leather
jackets abound. As in the show, sexual roles are polarized.

I glance down my row to where Emma is seated with
her parents. Their eyes are riveted on the stage. When the
band breaks into "Sherry," the Livelys smile. They know
this music well. Hit piles on hit, but the story line is heart-
felt. When Frankie Valli's daughter dies, the audience joins
him in his grief. When his partner runs up a million-dollar
debt, Valli bails him out, loyal to the teeth—and all on a
handshake deal, "Jersey style." The audience takes pride in
his loyalty.

I love the show but have one reservation. Bob Crewe,
who not only wrote the lyrics but also discovered and
produced the band, is played as a flamboyant queen. His
over-the-top homosexuality is used as comic relief. In real

life, Crewe is not effeminate. I wonder how he feels about his depiction. Perhaps he feels that it's for the good of the show: entertainment.

At show's end, the crowd jumps to its feet. The standing ovation feels well earned. As the song says, "I can't take my eyes off of you."

A sunny morning with music to match. Emma is at the piano, picking and pounding out melodies for *The Blue Lobster*. The show opens with a bravura a cappella turn for the great blue heron, and Emma is writing it with our friend Judy Collins in mind.

"She's the voice I have in my head. Anyone else will be a letdown, but do you think Judy would want to climb into a harness and fly onstage eight times a week?"

"No, I don't think so."

"But maybe she could record our demo. That would be amazing."

"Yes, it certainly would be."

"Judy even looks like a great blue heron."

"She does."

"We open with the heron alone and singing. When I told Judy about the flying idea, she said, 'I've done that before.' Nothing seems to daunt her."

"Yes, she's courageous. I think it's fine to write with her in mind. It sets the standard."

Emma dreams large, and Judy does, too. It occurs to me that Judy could be prerecorded. Someone else could be strapped into the harness to fly to the rafters. Of course, I am being practical. Emma and Judy dream on.

"What do you think of this?" Emma calls out. She plays a new melody that broadens out to a rock anthem.

"It's Elton John again," I tell her.

"I didn't steal it, though?" Emma is suddenly paranoid.

"No, it's original," I reassure her.

"I love Elton John. That's a great compliment," Emma

calls back. "See what you think of this." She ripples into yet another melody.

"I love it. The whole show is so melodic," I exclaim.

"I'm so glad you think so!" Emma says. When she plays the piano, both dogs creep close, listening with rapt attention. This is a high compliment. I call Tiger Lily "music dog" because she once nipped a bad piano player. But she loves Bob McDonald and Chaim Freiberg, creeping so close she almost blocks the piano pedals. Now with Emma at the keys she looks happy, basking in the music as she would in a spot of sunshine. Charlotte takes her cue from Tiger Lily. Her short tail brushes back and forth.

"You've got an audience," I tease Emma.

It's Tuesday, which means it's my day to have dinner with Tracy. It's gray and spitting rain, so I venture out with a hat and an umbrella. Tracy, bareheaded, waits for me just outside of Jackson Hole.

"Hello. You could have gone inside," I greet her.

"I hate sitting alone," she responds. "I'd rather wait for you out here, even in the rain."

We enter the café and take our usual corner table. The waitress knows our order by heart. We have bowls of cucumber-yogurt soup. I have an iced cappuccino.

"You first," Tracy urges me.

"I'm writing," I tell her. "I'm writing and reading. I wish I were going faster, but I'm managing a daily drib or drab. And you?"

"I made out my will and so did my husband. I suppose it's normal that it caused me a depression."

"Yes. I suppose so."

"But it did feel responsible, and that felt good."

"Yes. I can see that."

"I'm not sure what to do next. I finished my rug-hooking project and I've only got a few restoration projects, none of them very fun."

"That's too bad."

"What really bugs me is not getting paid in a timely fashion. I hate it when I have to nag."

Tracy goes on to catalog recent projects where her paycheck was delayed.

"I know these people have plenty of money, so it makes me feel really petty asking for what is really a modest amount."

I commiserate with her plight. I just had the devil's own time securing my paycheck for some teaching. Today—finally—my money arrived, but not without a lot of e-mail nagging.

"My apartment is crammed with projects—old projects, new projects, potential projects," Tracy relates. "Every surface is covered with art-in-the-making. Sometimes I just look at it and feel overwhelmed. Other times I will think, *Hey, I could work on—*"

Tracy unknots her hand-knitted scarf. She adjusts the handmade necklace that touches her collarbones. Both the

scarf and the necklace are exquisite—she made them both—
and both would be very expensive if they were to be sold at
retail prices. Almost always, Tracy is wearing a handmade
something—a pin, a scarf, a necklace—and almost always
she wears something sage green, her best color. Today she
wears a purple turtleneck with a sage jacket, the colors of
New Mexico. A tall and tawny blonde, she cuts a striking
figure. With her long strides, she looks like the athlete that
she is. Each morning she goes for a run in Riverside Park.
Each weekend she rides her horse, Fifty.

"Fifty is getting old," she laments. "His hindquarters
are weak. We have to take it easy."

Plainly, Tracy doesn't like "taking it easy." I remember
her cantering through the woods in Central Park. I remember her flying through traffic on her roller skates. It occurs
to me that Tracy must hold similar images of me. I no longer own a horse, and I no longer roller-skate. Tracy and
I hold each other's daredevil history. Our adventures now
are artistic, not physical.

"I've got an idea for a rug I'd like to hook," Tracy announces. The rug is of her horse, Fifty, young and vigorous.

"Do it," I urge her.

The first snow of the season is falling in damp flurries. Streets glisten. Windows glow. I turn into the small door-way to the vegetarian café. The waiter smiles and shows me to a corner table where Peter's scarf and jacket festoon a chair. I slip into my empty place. Peter looms suddenly close. His hair curls in ringlets from the weather. He leans in to give me a kiss.

"Hello. It's good to see you," I greet him.

"It's good to see you, too," he responds.

The waiter approaches our table.

"The usual?" he asks.

"Yes, for me," Peter answers. "I'll have the Zen platter."

"For me, too," I offer. "But extra tofu and no seitan."

The waiter retreats but is back with our salads in hand a moment later. He places a bowl of ginger dressing between us. The salads are large and fresh. I eat mine voraciously. Peter picks more carefully at his.

"I'm having trouble writing," I volunteer.

"Why does this sound familiar?" Peter counters.

"No. Really. It's uphill these days."

"You've written how many books? Thirty?"

"Something like that."

"So you'll write this one."

"I hope so."

"You'll write it."

The waiter whisks away our salad plates and returns with our Zen platter, two plates heaped with tofu, kale, couscous, and more salad. I attack the kale, sautéed with garlic. Peter slices delicately at his seitan. He is a picky eater and has to work consciously to keep his weight up. I feel like a plump partridge by comparison.

"When my apartment sells—soon, God willing—I am going to room with Jerry Brody for a while."

Brody is Peter's acting coach and a thoroughly nice man. Peter himself is a nice man, so the household should be harmonious.

"That sounds good," I tell Peter, happy that he has a definite landing pad. He is selling the apartment he grew up in, and there are a great deal of memories and identity attached to it. But his monthly nut is nearly six thousand dollars, and he yearns for a life with less financial pressure. Selling his apartment would allow him to live more comfort-ably but selling it is a wrenching loss, despite the gains.

"Let's have dessert this week," I propose.

"We could do that."

The waiter overhears us and offers a list of our options, ranging from pumpkin pie to blueberry flan. I select a slice of banana cream pie. It arrives with two forks, the better to share.

"Do you think this is a restaurant for eccentrics?" I ask

Peter. He laughs, glancing around at our fellow diners, a motley crew.

"You could be right," he concedes.

When I open my door to Bob McDonald, the dogs whirl in happiness around his feet. I feel like doing the same thing. Bob is a household favorite.

"Well, hello," he greets the dogs, chuckling at their antics.

"Hello to you," I say. "Down, girls."

Reluctantly, the dogs obey, although they still eddy around his knees as he steps inside.

"This is much better," Bob says, nodding to our newly rearranged living room. "It feels much larger."

"Yes, now the piano says, 'Play me.'"

"Oh, no, not that." Bob laughs. He has already put in long hours at his piano and then longer hours coaching his students. As the season turns, the deadline approaches for judging next year's entrants to Juilliard. From four hundred tapes, a handful will be selected, but all four hundred tapes must be carefully listened to. The task looms ahead of Bob. In the telling, it seems insurmountable, and yet it will get done.

Over the past few years, I have found Bob's workload to be staggering. He is on the faculty of Juilliard and on the faculty for the Curtis Institute of Music. At both schools, he carries a full load of students. Additionally, Bob travels and tours with Midori, juggling his teaching chores to accommodate his performance career. Although he loves teaching, and loves the caliber of students he's getting, his heart goes to the high-wire act of live performance.

It has been my great good fortune to listen to Bob's piano skills in solo concerts as well as duets. His playing has passion and clarity. He somehow conveys the architecture of the pieces he plays. He says modestly that he is merely trying to play the composers' intention. Listening to him play, the genius of the composers shines through. Bob has a genuine love for music. In his few "off" hours, he attends operas and concerts. His love of music shimmers off of him. Tiger Lily, our "music dog," is besotted with him. She curls at his feet.

"That a girl," Bob croons, bending down to give her a pat.

"She loves you," I say.

"Well, it's mutual," says Bob. "Isn't it, girl?"

Laughter pries its way under my bedroom door. Emma and Domenica are baking a Spider-Man cake for Bunny's Bakery. The cake involves a complicated mold and then complex frosting with five different colors. Emma frosts the web using black frosting. Domenica does the costume using red. While they work, they play the Rolling Stones' *Let It*

Bleed. Domenica sings along, remembering the words from when she was little and I played the album as I wrote.

It's a lean year for Bunny's Bakery. Regular orders are smaller. Some clients don't order at all. Others pare their orders down to the bare minimum. Emma is still braced to be slammed with last-minute holiday requests, but so far she and Domenica are keeping easily abreast.

"This is happy," Domenica declares, lifting a chocolate-peppermint cookie onto a cooling rack. "This is very, very happy."

Domenica is glad to be working and takes great delight in a job well done. With the baking, there is a tangible beginning, middle, and end. Not only are the cookies, cakes, and pies delicious, they are also beautifully presented. Domenica, a Virgo to her fingertips, enjoys fussing, making each order "perfect."

Emma, the mastermind behind the bakery, is delighted to share the workload with another. Last year she did everything herself, and she was in tears from the stress. No tears this year, just laughter. It is a luxury for me having both Emma and Domenica under one roof—my favorites, I tell them.

And they are baking my favorites, too.

To date, they have baked six different kinds of cookies—gingersnaps, shortbread, peppermint-chocolate, almond–white chocolate–cherry, butterscotch chip, chocolate-oatmeal-raisin—and pink-and-white–frosted brownies. They have baked Spider-Man and an elaborate gingerbread house; they have orders in for a chocolate-peppermint cake and a ginger cake with chocolate ganache. They will probably bake the whole weekend through.

"He looks pretty good, doesn't he?" asks Emma, gesturing to the Spider-Man cake nestled in a special box.

"I think it looks great," I tell her. "That is one lucky birthday boy."

"Is he five?" Domenica asks.

"No, he's only three, but his mother says he's obsessed with Spider-Man." Emma puts three candles in the box.

"Well, then, he should be happy with it," says Domenica.

"What kind of cake?" I ask.

"Chocolate with vanilla frosting, his favorite," Emma answers.

The doorbell rings. I open it to Sara Carder, my editor at Tarcher/Penguin and the proud mom who ordered the Spider-Man cake.

"Oh, it's wonderful!" Sara exclaims. "Not that I'm competitive, but that's the best birthday cake I've seen among his friends."

"Cut the box apart. Don't try to lift it out," Emma instructs, "and keep it level until you get it home. Then refrigerate it."

"Thanks again. I just love it." Sara takes the cake.

"I'm so glad," says Emma.

"Thank you," says Sara. Emma shows her to the door, then turns to Domenica, who laughs with glee. "It's so satisfying when someone loves what we've done," she exclaims.

The cab pulls up to the curb at 78 Fifth Avenue. "East West Living," the script beside the doorway reads. I pay the driver and hurry into the shop. I am due to do a book signing in fifteen minutes. The occasion is the paperback publication of my novel *Mozart's Ghost*.

The shop is two stories, and the signing is to be held on the second floor in the café. They have set up a special table for me, featuring stacks of my books ready to be purchased. I set my coat and purse to one side and settle into the speaker's chair. The room is crowded, and I recognize some of my students, past and present. It feels a little like we're playing hooky, seeing one another outside of class. Cami, the events coordinator, tells me we will wait an extra five minutes for the stragglers. "You know how New Yorkers are, always late."

Five minutes, four, three, two, one, zero. I open my remarks by thanking everyone for coming out on such a cold and blustery night. "I thought I'd begin by telling you the circumstances this book got written in. I wrote the book while I was out on book tour. I made a rule for myself that it had to be entirely made with ingredients from my own life—no research necessary. So Anna, our heroine, lives in my apartment building, eats at my favorite diner, walks my neighborhood streets. Edward, our hero, is tailored after a writer friend of mine. I fell in love with him, but in life nothing came of it. In the book, I turned him into a pianist and got my happily ever after."

The crowd chuckles at my tale of unrequited love. "Does he know he's the character?" one woman asks.

"No, I don't think so," I answer. "He's read the book and given me notes on it, but he never said, 'Ah! That's me.'"

I explain my writing process: first longhand, then computer; first friends, then critics. I explain the process I call "green sheets," a dense and careful outline that allows me to make changes without getting lost.

"Do you think your longhand pages have anything to do with your Morning Pages?" I am asked.

"Yes, I think they do. Morning Pages taught me freedom of expression. My inner critic learned to stand aside.

Writing the novel longhand gave me such freedom. 'Stand aside,' I command my critic. Trained from the Morning Pages, my critic obeyed . . . or at least obeyed more often than when I was working at the computer."

A beautiful black woman seated in the first row asks me if I'd had a spiritual experience that had influenced my writing technique.

"Yes," I tell her. "In 1978, I got sober and I needed to find a way to write sober. I learned to let myself write freely, allowing the higher power to write through me. I became less the self-conscious author and more the conduit. Instead of thinking something up, I learned to take something down. The direction was important. Thinking something up could imply strain. Taking something down was more like dictation."

There is a pause in the questioning, and so I read a section from the book. When I finish, there is a warm round of applause. The audience connects with Anna. They are rooting for her, just as I'd hoped. Next, I read the section on Anna's meditation practice. Again, I am met with applause. I explain that Anna's life as a medium is grounded in the real-life details of my friends Sonia Choquette and Larry Lonergan. I tell the audience about another medium who read the book and called me to say, "It's so realistic. It's just like my life."

In the name of realism, I read a chapter of Anna at a tropical-fish store where the clerk is flirting with her. Again the audience bursts into applause. On that high note, I move out of questions and answers and into the actual signing. Sales are brisk, with one woman buying five books, four for Christmas presents. I know that the sale of my sequel to the novel hinges on how well the sales go on *Mozart's Ghost* in paperback. I hope for the best, signing each book carefully. Each sale is a gift.

I wake to the scent of gingerbread baking. Emma is making a gingerbread house for her agent. It takes fifty minutes for the cake to bake. Before it is done, the scent wafts through the apartment. It smells delicious.

"Oh, no! I don't believe it!" Emma's exclamation echoes from room to room.

"What is it?" I carol back to her.

"I dropped the cake! It shattered!" Emma calls back.

"It's broken?" I ask. "What a catastrophe!"

"Yes, it's completely ruined. I'll have to bake another one," Emma laments. She brings a cookie sheet laden with the bits of broken cake into my room. I reach out and snag a piece. Her gingerbread houses are always delicious—but not this one! Its flavor is too strong.

"This tastes different than usual," I comment. "It's not as good."

Emma samples a bite and makes a grimace. "I used a different brand of molasses," she explains. "It's good the cake broke. I'll make another one with my usual brand of molasses. This one isn't up to par."

From the relief in her voice I can tell Emma felt she'd had a close call. Bunny's Bakery prides itself on baked goods that both look and taste delicious. The marred gingerbread house wasn't up to Bunny's standards.

"Everything happens for a purpose," our friend Jennifer Bassey exclaims when I tell her about the dropped cake later in the day.

"Yes, she caught her mistake in the nick of time," I say.

"Yes, and she'd never dropped anything before?" Jennifer asks.

"No, never."

"Well, then—" Jennifer clearly sees a small miracle. "God wanted her attention."

There is a light knock at the door. I almost don't hear it. The knock comes again. I open the door to greet Ben Lively, Emma's brother. He is laden with two suitcases, a briefcase for his computer, and a violin. For more than a year he has been living on the road with the touring company of *Spring Awakening*. We will have him for five days.

"Hello!" Emma sings out.

"Hello," Ben answers back. He engulfs her in a brotherly bear hug.

"You've got enough stuff!"

"Should I put it in here?" Ben hauls his gear to our extra room.

"That's perfect," Emma assures him.

"Bunny's Bakery is going full tilt," he observes.

"So far we're keeping abreast."

"Hi." Domenica steps from the kitchen.

"Hi, there," Ben greets her. "You're the help?"

"I am," she confirms, gesturing to a tower of boxes she has prepped for cookies.

"We've got twenty-four boxes of cookies, eleven dozen cupcakes, and five cakes," Emma announces. "We're trying to stay on top of the orders. So far so good." She cues up Cyndi Lauper's greatest hits, and Domenica sings along, letter-perfect on the lyrics.

Stepping into the kitchen, Emma spoons dough onto a cookie sheet. With extra care, she slides the sheet into the oven. No more accidents! She readies a second tray. And a third. By now, the first tray is ready to come out. "Looking good!" Emma exclaims.

"Looking good," Domenica echoes. She sets about gently prying the cookies loose and setting them on a cooling rack. "Yikes, I broke one!"

"I'll have to eat it!" says Ben.

"Ready for more?" Emma asks as she slides out another cookie sheet. Deftly and carefully, Domenica sets each cookie to cool.

"What about the Rolling Stones?" Domenica asks. Now she sings along with Mick Jagger. She knows every word.

"Anyone else getting hungry?" Emma asks. "I'm thinking Shake Shack."

"That's perfect," Ben announces.

"Yes, it's ranked number one in our greasy burger-tasting contest," says Emma.

I've never been to Shake Shack, so I am up for an

adventure. Bundled head to toe, the four of us set out to walk ten blocks south. We pass many windows dressed for Christmas.

"The windows on Fifth Avenue aren't as good as usual this year," Domenica pronounces. Yesterday, she walked thirty blocks, window-shopping.

"In London we went to Harrods, and their windows were all scenes from *The Wizard of Oz*. There was the yellow brick road, ruby slippers, the Tin Man, and the Scarecrow. Oh, yes, and Toto. They were wonderful," I tell Domenica.

We arrive at Shake Shack, which is crammed, standing room only. Emma goes down to the basement rec room, where she scores us a standing table. All four of us order double Shake Shack burgers and french fries. Our orders come up, and we ferry them to our table, where we devour our burgers in great, greasy gulps. Domenica and I swig at our Arnold Palmers, half lemonade, half iced tea. We don't finish our drinks. They are more than generous.

"All set?" Emma asks as we clear our trays. She is the ringleader, and Bunny's is calling.

"All set," I answer.

"Yep," says Ben.

"I'm ready," says Domenica. We climb back to street level. Noses into the wind, we hike the ten blocks back to Bunny's Bakery. There are four dozen cupcakes yet to go.

My friend Gerard is playing host. He has invited us—myself; Emma; and Emma's brother, Ben—to a concert staged by the students of his Upper West Side music school. The ages range from four to twelve. The venue is Merkin Hall. The students of his school are handpicked for their musical abilities. Last year, four hundred youngsters auditioned for fourteen slots. Gerard is justifiably proud of the students' acumen.

The lights dim and a troupe of tiny students climb onstage. They are the kindergarten eurythmics class, and they have prepared two numbers. Their voices ring out clear and bell-like. "Winter is coming," they sing. "The weather is changing. Mornings are frosty and evenings are chill." Their diction is clear, no mean feat for such young voices. They finish to a warm round of applause. The concert is off to a good start. For the next ninety minutes we are well entertained. There is joy and pride on the students' faces as they take their turns. Under the direction of Sean Hartley and Emily John, the choral numbers are crisp and tuneful. Gerard beams as the afternoon unfolds.

"Shall we go for coffee?" Gerard asks after the final round of applause.

"We were thinking Chinese," says Emma.

"Fine by me," Gerard concedes.

And so Emma, Ben, Gerard, Gerard's sister Virginia, and I troop the block and a half to Ollie's, a Chinese restaurant.

"I'm so glad you were able to come," Gerard says, addressing the table. "I think it's special, and I'm glad to be able to share it."

Emma and Ben order large bowls of wonton soup with extra noodles and spinach. I order cold soba noodles with peanut sauce. Gerard has a glass of chardonnay, and Virginia a glass of merlot.

"We're a public school," Gerard explains, "and I think we're the only school in the country where students get two forty-five-minute lessons of individual music instruction a week."

"That's a lot," says Emma, who holds a master's degree in viola performance. "That's great."

"It is a lot," concurs Ben, highly trained as a jazz violinist.

"I'm taking piano and I do one lesson a week," I say. "I'd never be ready to do a second one."

"Yes, well, our parents are a big help," says Gerard. "They take the music homework seriously."

"Maybe I need to borrow a parent," I joke.

It's nine p.m., and Bunny's Bakery is going full tilt. Domenica constructs a stack of hot-pink boxes. Our neighbor, Cara Quinn, cuts lengths of ribbon to tie the boxes securely shut. Emma bends over a tray of cupcakes, frosting gun in one hand. She meticulously frosts each cupcake, then sprinkles colored sugar as a final touch.

"Let's listen to Cyndi Lauper again," Domenica suggests. Emma cues it up. Again, Lauper's unique voice fills the apartment. Again, Domenica sings along. As her boyfriend has noted to me, she has a wonderful voice. It is husky and distinctive.

"There. That's the very last one," Emma exclaims, straightening to survey her handiwork. The cupcakes look, frankly, glorious. Bunny's Bakery has done it again.

" 'Time after time,' " carols Cyndi Lauper.

" 'Time after time,' " Domenica echoes.

"Now, how are we going to package these?" Emma asks Domenica, who has shown a knack for festive wrappings. Domenica takes a sheet of wrapping paper and folds it neatly into thirds. It fits perfectly into the boxes. The cupcakes perch carefully on the wrapping paper, and the final third folds over.

"Shall we give it the Bunny's Bakery seal of fresh-ness?" Domenica asks.

"Of course," I say, and so Domenica carefully affixes a gold sticker to the wrapping paper holding the cupcakes.

She announces her satisfaction. "There. That should do it."

"Everything looks so beautiful," Cara states.

"Yes, we try for 'tastes good, looks good,'" Emma responds.

"There's something very satisfying in a job well done," says Domenica.

Cara is a producer. Emma is a composer. Domenica is a writer-director-actor. They could make a documentary on Bunny's Bakery. They each wear an apron and a toque.

"Girls just want to have fun," sings Cyndi Lauper.

Listening to the laughter at Bunny's Bakery, it certainly seems she's got it right.

"I think of it as playing Treasure Hunt," says Domenica. Her boyfriend is a gourmet cook, so he keeps sending her out for exotic ingredients: caraway seeds, a yellow pepper, caviar. For the most part she manages to find them. This is Manhattan, where almost anything can be found.

"He says he has no sweet tooth, but he gobbled up all the gingersnaps I brought home to him," Domenica goes on. "Maybe he just likes good sweets," she speculates.

Domenica is still in the discovery phase with her boyfriend. Everything about him is new and fascinating. His skill as a chef is just one new variable. His four years of living in Paris left him with a wealth of information about all things French.

To hear her tell it, they are enjoying a long, happily unfurling conversation. "This is a man with opinions. Sometimes I disagree with him, and then I'll say, 'Really?'"

It's a Friday night, and Domenica has met me for dinner. We sit at the window of Bella Luna, starved for a good meal and a good long catch-up. Domenica is wearing a beret that I gave her. It has a flower perched on one temple, very glamorous. With her sooty eyelashes and serene oval face, Domenica is a classic beauty. The waiter is charmed by her. She orders her usual salmon carpaccio, while I order my usual skirt steak. We split an order of mezzo.

As she talks about her relationship, I find myself listening for the *but*, as in, "He was wonderful, *but* . . ." It doesn't seem that there is a *but*. Domenica's new boyfriend may actually be just as nice as she is.

I wonder if he keeps waiting for Domenica to show a sour side. If so, he'll have a long wait. She is genuinely supportive. In meeting Domenica, he has lucked out. If the same could be said of her luck finding him, they may make a good match. Domenica seems to think they do.

"You just like him," I sum up the conversation.

"Yes, I do," answers Domenica. "I do. I do."

I'm still in my pajamas when the phone rings. I dive to answer it. It is my friend James Dybas, just checking in and wondering if I'd like to meet for a sandwich.

"Give me twenty minutes," I propose.

"Fine," says James. "I'll meet you at the Greek diner on your corner."

"Great. See you there," I say.

I fly to the mirror and put on my makeup. I work quickly but well. Makeup done, I slip into black slacks and a slithery black top. I look presentable enough. James always looks dapper. I don't want him to look like he's gone slumming.

At the diner, James has snared a table for two. He's downing a bowl of minestrone soup. He stops mid-spoonful to welcome me. I have a flash of pride. James is very hand-some. It's fun to be seen with him, like wearing a pair of diamond studs with blue jeans. Who am I trying to impress? The world, evidently. James is a "Broadway perennial," according to Bruce Pomahac, music director for Rodgers and Hammerstein. Even if you don't recognize him or know his credits, James has an extra dollop of charisma. He all but glows.

"How was your week?" he asks me.

"Oh, medium," I reply. "I'm writing but slowly."

James nods in sympathy. A full-time actor, he has tried his hand at writing, too. Yes, he knows it can be difficult.

"How was your week?" I counter, knowing that he has been fighting flu and a bronchial infection.

"Well, I'm not coughing anymore," he answers.

"No, you seem much better. Your color is better, too."

James had been ghostly pale but now no longer.

"I'm singing Christmas Eve," he volunteers. I hope by then he will be totally well.

James loves his work, and even talking about singing causes him to brighten perceptibly. He has sung on three of Emma's and my demos. Even among fellow Broadway talents, his performances stand out.

The waiter comes hovering. I order a BLT, in honor of my heroine Anna from *Mozart's Ghost*. Much of the novel is set at this diner, and I half expect Anna to walk in as James orders a tuna salad.

"What happened on Emma's latest trip to Chicago? Was it a success?" James asks me. "She goes so often, I can hardly keep up with her."

"Neither can I. But I think she's making real progress on all of the projects."

"That's great."

"This trip was a surprise, though. Our director, David Bell, told us he wanted to do another play of mine first. It's called *Love in the DMZ*, and it took prizes when it was put on out in Los Angeles. I think it may be a stronger play than *The Medium at Large*, but I don't want to give up on *The Medium*."

"That is a jolt," James concedes. "But it might be a good thing. What do you think?"

"I'm trying not to think," I joke. "I'm trying to just go with the flow. Maybe it's right, leading off with a more serious play."

"How big a cast?"

"Two."

"That's what they're looking for."

"Yes. Maybe."

"It's good timing for a Vietnam play. Lots of parallels."

"Yes, it may be good timing." I name two Chicago actors currently reading the script.

"They'd be great."

"Yes, I think so."

"Two Chicagoans."

"Yes, and I'm a Chicagoan, too."

"Me, too. All good people," he jokes.

James hurries his sandwich. He is due on the East Side in twenty minutes. I reach for my wallet, but he waves me off. "My treat," he says.

"Thank you. I feel thoroughly spoiled," I tell him. We kiss good-bye.

It is a chill, gray day, and once again we are driving north from New York City to Wilton, Maine. The trip is four hundred miles and usually takes eight hours, but today is not usual. It takes us three and a half hours just to get to New Haven. Traffic is dense and slow. In order to pass the time, we cue up album after album. My favorite is Frankie Valli and The Four Seasons. I particularly love "December 1963 (Oh, What a Night)."

"I just love this song," I say to Emma.

"Me, too. It's my favorite," Emma replies.

"He just has the greatest voice. His range is awesome."

"Yes, Frankie Valli is the best."

Frankie Valli is so good he makes us forget the tortoise crawl of the holiday traffic. We are invited to stop for tea at Emma's Aunt Jackie and Uncle Bill Capp's house outside of Boston. The traffic is so slow that we arrive at their house at dinnertime. They welcome us in with open arms.

Our "tea" is laid out: a variety of cheeses, fruits, and guaca-
mole with chips. We're hungry after the day in the car.

I am eager to take a tour of the house. Aunt Jackie is a
painter, and I've never seen her work. That oversight is soon
remedied. There are three portraits hung prominently in the
entryway. They are not just good. They are remarkable.

"Yes, these are mine," Aunt Jackie confesses mod-
estly. She leads us up a few steps to a wonderful studio.
"This is my guilt room," she laments. "I keep telling myself
I will get in here and paint."

"I hope you will. You're incredibly gifted."

"Thanks. That means a lot."

"Have you thought of doing a portrait of your daughter, Lauren?" I ask her. Lauren is a particularly beautiful
young woman.

"Yes, I have," says Jackie. "Here are two pencil stud-
ies I've done of her." She lays out two sketches that are
wonderful.

"These are great," I say.

Suddenly, there is a growl and some high-pitched yelping. My dog, Tiger Lily, has attacked Jackie's little bichon frise. I grab Tiger Lily by the collar.

"That's enough, girl!" I tell her.

Jackie's dog is unharmed but a bit rattled. I snap Tiger Lily onto her leash. She clearly would love to get another fluffy mouthful.

"Maybe it's time we get going," I suggest. Emma is reluctant to leave, but leave we do. Charlotte, Emma's dog, has behaved beautifully, but she's tarred by the same brush as Tiger Lily. We hustle both dogs into the car.

"A pretty house, isn't it?" Emma asks as we pull out of the drive.

"Yes, a very pretty house," I answer. By comparison, our New York City apartment is cramped and crammed.

"Settle down, girls," I say to the dogs as we swing back onto the highway. Our next stop is the Portland bus station, where we are picking up Ben. Because we are running late, he has been waiting an extra hour. He has used that hour to send Emma multiple text messages, telling her to hurry up and accusing her of "playing too long at the Capps'." Emma is driving, and so I report on Ben's barrage.

"Tell him I'm driving ninety miles an hour," Emma snorts.

"I hate this iPhone, I don't know how to work it. And don't speed," I tell her, putting the phone down.

At the bus station, Emma goes inside to retrieve Ben. He slings his gear into the back of the car, then slides into the driver's seat. An excellent driver who loves to drive, he will pilot the last leg to Maine.

"Mum's been worrying about snow, but the coast looks clear," Ben announces. He shifts smoothly into gear and points the car north. An hour and a half later, we cross the line into Wilton. As we do, a flurry of snowflakes suddenly appears.

"We'll have to tell Mum, no snow until we got to Wilton," Ben jokes. He turns on the wipers and slows the car to a crawl for the last few turns before—voilà!—home sweet home.

"My family has gotten you an awesome present," Emma teases me. "But Mum says I'm not to talk to you about it or you will guess."

"So don't talk to me," I tease back. My best guess for an awesome present is an espresso-making machine. The Livelys know I love cappuccino. Other than the espresso machine, I come up blank. Emma is positively smug. She mentions the "awesome" gift several times, but my ESP is on the fritz. I can't guess with any accuracy.

The Lively Christmas tree is full and beautiful. It is hung with distinctive, whimsical ornaments. Under its boughs, the presents are piled high. I have brought the Livelys a giant poinsettia and a gingerbread house. They have gotten me an "awesome" gift. Gently, I lift the box that contains my present. It's too light to be an espresso machine.

"Open it, open it!" the Livelys urge. It is Christmas

Eve, not Day, but they don't want me to wait. Gingerly, I tear open the wrappings. I open the box to more wrappings. Something is fragile, but what? At last I reach the gift itself. It takes my breath away.

"Oh, wow!" I breathe.

"Lift it out!" Emma urges.

Very carefully, I lift the gift—a hand-carved duck decoy. It is beautiful. I recognize the bird as a female teal duck, so named for the teal feathers at its wing tips.

"This is incredible," I exclaim. I gently heft the bird. "But how did you ever?" Last August I had seen the bird, one of a kind, at the home of the Livelys' friends, Joan and Dave Haeger, who had just started carving decoys as a hobby. "Is this for sale?" I had asked, feeling my fingertips tingle as they touched the little bird.

"No, I'm afraid it's not for sale," Dave replied.

Somehow, between August and December, the Livelys had persuaded him to sell. The bird was now mine. Gently, I stroked its back, each feather carefully articulated.

"It's just incredible," I breathe.

"I told you it was an awesome present," Emma gloats.

"Much better than an espresso machine," I say.

"That's what you thought it would be?" asks Rob.

"It was the only thing I could think of," I say. "But this is a hundred times better."

"It won a blue ribbon in a carving contest," volunteers Martha.

"It deserves a blue ribbon," I respond. "And it deserves a name, too." My late father collected decoys. When he died, I inherited a set of brass bookends in the shape of ducks. My apartment is filled with Audubon prints: owls, blue herons, woodpeckers, and hawks. I have a small collection of decoys that sits on top of the piano. The new little decoy will join them there.

"I was afraid you would guess," says Martha.

"I never would have guessed," I tell her. "After all, I knew the bird was not for sale. How on earth did you convince him?"

"Lively charm," kids Emma. "And everyone knew how much you loved it." I turn the bird in my hands.

"And I do love it. It's signed on the bottom, 'Dave and Joan Haeger, number one.'" I turn the bird right side up.

"I think I'll call her Martha," I say. "Like Martha Lively, brilliant but subtle."

It's a gray day full of sleet and bad weather. The roads are slick, plagued by black ice. We decide to stay in rather than go out to the movies. We've rented the DVD of *Julie & Julia*. I've seen it before but am eager to see it again. As the day darkens toward evening, we cue it up.

The movie opens with a dining adventure. Newly arrived in France, Julia Child and her husband, Paul, seek out a perfect French meal: sole meunière. As played by Meryl Streep, Julia Child has a voracious appetite for life. She savors life as delicious, particularly as embodied by

French cuisine. When she enrolls at the Cordon Bleu, it is a stroke of destiny.

Curled up on the Livelys' couch, Martha and I laugh out loud at some of the film's gentle humor. Ephron's script is deft and engaging. As with the real Julia Child, the movie is haute cuisine made accessible.

And it is. Meryl Streep and Stanley Tucci are delicious as Julia Child and her husband, Paul. Their story is a love story, and it's tonic to see Nora's sophisticated take on it. Amy Adams plays Julie, the young wife who cooks her way all the way through Child's *Mastering the Art of French Cooking*. She files a daily blog reporting on her experience. We root for her to succeed. Cutting back and forth between the two couples and their stories, Nora crafts a deft romantic comedy.

"Have you ever used her cookbook?" I ask Martha as the credits roll.

"Yes, yes, I have," she answers.

I tell Martha about giving Child's cookbook to my

little sister, Lorrie, when she was still a teenager. As I recall, every dish that she made from it was delicious.

"It's quite good," I conclude. "And I think the film's good, too."

I tell Martha that Nora Ephron's career is one that I envy. "But I'm still rooting for her," I explain. During our twenties, as fledgling writers, Nora and I were friends. Our later lives took us in differing directions. I became a book writer, and she turned to films. I wrote and directed one feature film, but then books took over. Nora has gone on to make film after film, and some of them are quite good. I tell myself movies are in her blood. Her parents were a successful screenwriting team. Nora inherited the movie DNA. Her films are well-written throwbacks to the age of great screen romantic comedies. I have a twinge of jealousy, and I say as much.

"Think of all the good your books have done," Emma continues, stubbornly optimistic.

"That's not the point," I protest.

"What is the point?" asks Martha.

"My jealousy. It tells me that I wish I were making movies, too."

"Really?"

"Yes, really." Nora's credits crawl to a halt. "Good movie," I say.

The night is icy cold. Arctic winds blast down the avenues. I am bundled in a fur coat topped by a soft wool muffler—and I'm still cold. I hurry up First Avenue to Peter's and my regular café. The wind pushes through the doorway with me. Peter looks up and smiles. "Hello." I slide into the empty chair across from him.

"Good to see you," he says.

We don't need menus. We order our usual vegetarian platters. The waiter remembers the extra tofu. He serves our salads with an extra side of ginger dressing.

"I've got an appetite tonight," Peter announces. We turn our attention to our salads, which are big and fresh.

"I saw a good movie," Peter volunteers. "I went to the movies New Year's Eve night and saw *It's Complicated*. Streep was great, but Alec Baldwin was laugh-out-loud funny. He's so expressive."

"I saw a good movie, too," I say. "*Julie and Julia*."

"I'm not interested in Julia Child."

"It's a good movie anyhow. The relationships are great."

Our waiter clears our salad plates and serves us our entrées.

"I forgot to bring a scene that I've written," Peter says. He dices up his tofu.

"So bring it next week. It would really be fun to play it." I enjoy Peter's acting forays.

"Well, it's shorter than the scene we did from *All My Sons*." Peter's modesty is engaging.

"I enjoyed reading it with you," I tell him.

"Yes, but I'm sure I'm no Arthur Miller."

"We'll see. Just remember to bring the scene."

"I can do that."

"Dessert?" our waiter offers. Peter and I both decline, opting for cups of Red Zinger tea. Sipping at the tea, we talk about our daughters, the good luck we both have that our girls are straight arrows.

I tell Peter I have dinner plans with Domenica for the next evening. It is a luxury, we both agree, having our daughters in the same city and "available for viewing."

The day is icy cold again. Wind rattles the windows of our apartment. Luckily, we are not going out. Instead, we have a dozen people dropping in. It is a first reading of Emma and Tyler's show, *The Blue Lobster*. Curtain is scheduled for three p.m., but a phone call from our leading lady asks us to excuse her tardiness. The subways are running late.

Emma's brother, Ben, has also hit travel snafus. It is four o'clock before the whole cast is assembled. For five days, Emma and Tyler have worked around the clock. Now they will see what they have.

Emma reads the stage directions. Tyler is at the piano, performing all the songs. The show rollicks along, number to number. The storytelling is clear and the show is well cast. The small audience claps and laughs. The first act runs forty-five minutes. At the act break there is a buzz of excitement. So far so good. Act two runs a swift thirty-one minutes. The show finishes with a flourish. For a first read-through, it is a success.

After the reading, we have a talkback, but there is very little criticism. Tyler and Emma are buoyed by the enthusiasm of the crowd. Asked if they can come up with any storytelling loopholes, the crowd doesn't find any. They give a green light to proceed to a second reading and a demo.

After the crowd has gone, Emma and Tyler hug each other with glee. The show unfolded better than they had hoped.

"I think they really liked it," Emma exclaims.

"Yes. It sure seemed like it," Tyler concurs.

"The show is fine," I tell them. "Don't go pulling it apart."

Domenica enters Bella Luna rosy-cheeked from cold. She stomps her feet and rubs her hands together.

"It's really cold out," she announces.

"That it is," I agree.

I have ordered frothy decaf cappuccinos. They arrive just as Domenica takes her seat.

"Yum," she says, sampling a sip. I have ordered mezzo for two. When the platter arrives, we attack it with relish.

"So how are you doing with your new editor?" I ask.

"First-rate," Domenica says, signaling a thumbs-up. Her first editor of her short was problem-prone. Her second editor loves the piece. "He has made it a poem," Domenica reports, clearly delighted. "He cut two exchanges that I may restore, but the essential piece is there."

Tim, our waiter, materializes. We order minestrone soup and skirt steak. We also ask for another round of cappuccinos.

I haven't seen Domenica since before Christmas. While I was up in Maine, her boyfriend's mother and aunt came to New York for Christmas. Gerard has already told me that they were charming, but I am eager to hear Domenica's take.

"Charming and intense," she reports. Between spoonfuls of minestrone, she sketches in the visit. It does sound both charming and intense, two words I might use to describe Domenica's boyfriend, as well.

"Gerard really liked them," I tell Domenica. In our family, Gerard's perspective is highly valued.

"That's great," Domenica says.

"Yes, he liked them very much."

"I'm so glad."

We order a tartufo for dessert. Spooning it down, divided between the two of us, we talk of our New Year's resolutions and our relief that 2009, a difficult year, is over. We agree that 2010 promises to be productive. We both have resolutions that center on increased productivity.

"I want to weigh less and work more," I summarize my resolves.

"That sounds good," Domenica antes up.

"I wonder if our family might also be described as 'charming and intense,'" I remark.

"Yes, I suppose we might," says Domenica. She lifts her second cappuccino, sporting a mustache made of foam.

"I suppose we might," I echo. I signal for the check.

Epilogue

It is New Year's Eve. Emma and Tyler have gone to Saint John the Divine to hear Judy sing. I have stayed home, feeling the need to be introspective, to cast a glance backward over my year and see what can be learned. The first thing that is apparent is that slowing down my pace has enabled me to see and appreciate the help given to me by others. My friends form a community, wishing me well. I, in my turn, wish them the best. Our friend is home from the hospital and receiving visitors. The turn of the year is a return to normalcy. I look to the future, grateful for the new colleagues I have encountered—grateful, too, for the graceful dance of old friends who offer both support and guidance. May I do the same.

Discover Julia Cameron's Creative Kingdom

To order call 1-800-788-6262 or visit our website at www.penguin.com

BOOKS IN THE ARTIST'S WAY SERIES

The Artist's Way
- ISBN 978-1-58542-147-3 (hardcover)
- ISBN 978-1-58542-146-6 (trade paper)
- ISBN 978-0-14-305825-0 (audio, CDs)

Walking in This World
ISBN 978-1-58542-261-6 (trade paper)

Finding Water
- ISBN 978-1-58542-463-4 (hardcover)
- ISBN 978-1-58542-777-2 (trade paper)

The Artist's Way Workbook
ISBN 978-1-58542-533-4 (trade paper)

The Artist's Way Morning Pages Journal
ISBN 978-0-87477-886-1 (trade paper)

The Complete Artist's Way
ISBN 978-1-58542-630-0 (hardcover)

The Artist's Way Every Day
ISBN 978-1-58542-747-5 (trade paper)

The Artist's Date Book
ISBN 978-0-87477-653-9 (trade paper)

Inspirations: Meditations from
The Artist's Way
ISBN 978-1-58542-102-2 (trade paper)

The Artist's Way Starter Kit
ISBN 978-1-58542-928-8 (trade paper)

The Artist's Way Creative Kingdom Collection
ISBN 978-1-58542-927-1 (trade paper)

OTHER BOOKS ON CREATIVITY

The Right to Write
ISBN 978-1-58542-009-4 (trade paper)

The Sound of Paper
ISBN 978-1-58542-354-5 (trade paper)

The Writing Diet
ISBN 978-1-58542-698-0 (trade paper)

The Vein of Gold
ISBN 978-0-87477-879-3 (trade paper)

The Writer's Life: Insights from The Right
to Write
ISBN 978-1-58542-103-9 (trade paper)

PROSPERITY

The Prosperous Heart
ISBN 978-1-58542-897-7 (hardcover)

PRAYER BOOKS

Answered Prayers
ISBN 978-1-58542-351-4 (trade paper)

Heart Steps
ISBN 978-0-87477-899-1 (trade paper)

Blessings
ISBN 978-0-87477-906-6 (trade paper)

Transitions
ISBN 978-0-87477-995-0 (trade paper)

Prayers to the Great Creator
- ISBN 978-1-58542-682-9 (hardcover)
- ISBN 978-1-58542-778-9 (trade paper)

BOOKS ON SPIRITUALITY

Faith and Will
ISBN 978-1-58542-714-7 (hardcover)

Prayers from a Nonbeliever
ISBN 978-1-58542-213-5 (hardcover)

MEMOIR

Floor Sample: A Creative Memoir
- ISBN 978-1-58542-494-8 (hardcover)
- ISBN 978-1-58542-557-0 (trade paper)

Watch Julia Cameron on Tarcher Talks
@ www.penguin.com/tarchertalks

For over two decades, Julia Cameron has
inspired scores of artists around the world.
These pocket-sized card decks enable readers
to access Cameron's great wisdom
wherever they are!

The Artist's Way
CREATIVITY CARDS!

Keep your creative well filled with these 64 gorgeous cards. Each four-color card contains a vital quote from Julia Cameron's classic bestseller, *The Artist's Way*. In addition, each card contains a different creative quality— pick any card and be inspired and lovingly guided by Julia's wise words. A perfect gift for the artist in your life, and for anyone who wants to live more creatively.

ISBN 978-0-39916-162-9

$15.95

Available September 27, 2012